THE MICROBLADING BIBLE

CORINNE ASCH

Copyright © 2016, Corinne Asch

All rights reserved. No part of this book may be used or reproduced in any manner whatsoever without the written permission of the Publisher and Author.

www.themicrobladingbible.com

www.lashandbrowlab.com

Book Design: Bluebobo

PREFACE

A while back, I took a 3-day course in microblading, and although the teacher was very good and very knowledgeable, I found the course, like all the courses I've taken, to be lacking in detailed information. I still had so many questions which were left unanswered.

I set out to find answers, but found there was nothing that could answer all my questions without taking yet another class and spending thousands of dollars more.

I emailed, messengered and Facebooked tons of people. I followed all the microblading boards, asked hundreds of questions and even discovered new ones I didn't know I had. Then, there were a lot of opposing viewpoints where both sides made sense. Opposing viewpoints for how to properly heal the brows, or whether to numb or not before the first strokes. I looked for books on the subject, but found only one that was so general in its information, but it was more of a pamphlet than a book, with very little usable information.

Thankfully, research is what I love to do when I'm not microblading someone's eyebrows. So, after a lot of exhaustive research, I was able to piece the puzzle together.

This book is the result of all of my research and is a detailed journal of all the things I've learned. By far the most helpful and informative were the women on the microblading Facebook groups. The women on these boards have been the kindest, most knowledgeable and most generous people I have met. They shared some tips and secrets you won't find in any training, no matter how good. They were so ready and willing to share their knowledge. A true sisterhood.

To all of you, I thank you.

Writing this book has been like taking an advanced class in microblading, it filled in a lot of gaps and answered many questions.

My hope is that it will do the same for you.

TABLE OF CONTENTS

1: What is Microblading? 1
   A new technology

2: Client Consultation 7
   Determining if you are right for each other

3: Client Forms 13
   All the legal forms you need

4: The Importance of Proper Sterilization 25
   Blood borne pathogens and OSHA regulations

5: Getting to Know the Fitzpatricks 41
   The skin's tones and undertones

6: Understanding Pigments 47
   Choosing the right modifiers for the right skin type

7: To Numb Or Not To Numb 55
   When, what and how to apply

8: Measuring The Brows 77
   The best techniques for symmetrical brows

9: Choosing the Right Blade for the Job 93
   Which blades to use for which skin types and outcomes

10: The Microblading Procedure 103
    Stretch, angle and flow

11: After Care 113
    The importance of proper care

12: The Healing Process 121
    What you and your client can expect

13: Courses and Trainers 125

CHAPTER 1
WHAT IS MICRO BLADING?

Microblading is a semi-permanent eyebrow procedure that is carried out by a qualified technician using a special hand-tool which houses extremely sharp needles positioned in a way that resembles and operates very much likes a blade.

The required pigment is deposited into the superficial dermis of the skin with the disposable microblade which allows the technician to create crisp hair strokes that resemble natural eyebrow hairs.

Microblading differs from conventional semi-permanent tattooing by the very fact that it is a manual procedure. When using a hand held microblade, the color is deposited closer to the surface than when a machine is used leaving very fine and crisp hair strokes with no spilling under the skin.

Microblading is an advanced technique that requires a fundamental training for permanent makeup with no less than 100 hours of basic course. You must be properly trained so that you can carry the proper liability insurance, which is indispensible in order to protect yourself and your client.

It is extremely important to check your state's requirements on licensing, education and sanitation.

Please do NOT attempt to microblade without proper training and insurance in place.

This book is intended to be used as a reference manual and as an adjunct to the physical training you've already received, not as a training manual on it's own. Getting the proper hands on training in a physical classroom is the first and most important step to learning microblading. There is no substitute for proper training.

DO NOT SKIP THIS VERY IMPORTANT STEP!

ARTICLE

What is microblading? Everything to know about this eyebrow trend

Rheana Murray
Sep. 5, 2016 at 5:08 AM
TODAY

Eyebrow trends come and go, from thin and sharp to bold and bushy a la Cara Delevingne and basically every other model who's been hot in the past few years.

But the lastest trend we can't get enough of is microblading, a new tattoo technique that fills brows out or reshapes them by drawing on tiny lines that look like individuals hairs.

We know what you're thinking: tattooed eyebrows? No way. But hear us out. "Microblading leaves brows looking natural, not scary", said Jen Terban-Hertell, co owner of East Side Ink, the celebrity-approved tattoo parlor in New York City.

"It sounds terrifying, and there's this stigma of grandma's blue arch eyebrows, but these are completely different," she told TODAY Style.

Microblading is done with a hand-held tool—"it looks like an X-ACTO knife made out of needles," she said—"that puts pigment into the skin, but doesn't go as deep as a normal tattoo would. It's also semi-permanent. Your microbladed brows should last between one and three years", Terban-Hertell said, adding that 18 months is typical for most of her clients.

The procedure differs depending where you go, but she sees people twice—once for an initial appointment and then once the brow has healed for a touch-up.

"The actual microblading is problably the shortest part of your appointment," Terban-Hertell said. "I spend a lot of time getting to know my clients and what they want, what's realistic for their face and then drawing on them to make sure they're happy with the shape."

"I work with the brow bone and the structure of the face and make sure the eyebrows are moving when you're making expressions and they're on the right part of your face," she added.

But be warned that microblading is more expensive than drawing your brows on every morning: prepare to spend at least $500 and that appears to be on the low end for the service. I don't need to warn you not to pick a technician by the price. Quality matters. It's also a bit painful, but nothing that would scare most people away. "it feels kind of like plucking," Terban-Hertell said, adding that she numbs the brow area before microblading (and, hey, maybe that's a small price to pay for having "eyebrows on fleek," but that's your call.)

The procedure is still relatively new to the United States, but Terban-Hertell suspects it's about to become a "craze." And if you follow any beauty buffs on Instagram or you've somehow stumbled upon the #microblading hashtag already, you might argue the craze has already begun.

"It's extremely poplular in other countries and just now getting popular in the states," she said. "Most of my clients haven't heard of it, or they're just hearing about it now. But in the next year or so, it's going to be all you're going to hear about. Terban-Hertell herself is just starting to see the impact the service has had on her clients, who find her mostly through word of mouth.

"When I started doing this, I thought it looked fun," she said. "But it's funny, the one thing I hear most often from my clients is that it's life-changing, which is not a quote I thought I would hear when talking about eyebrows."

"There are women who won't leave the house if their eyebrows aren't drawn in," the artist added. "Or they'll avoid certain activities like a beach day or something that will cause their brow to sweat off or wipe off. But (after microblading) they can go to the pool or to Bikram yoga or whatever it is. This has turned out to be so rewarding because it changes the way people feel about themselves.

CHAPTER 2
CLIENT CONSULTATION

This is where the journey begins.

You meet, you talk about expectations and limitations. You analyze her skin, her medical history and, finally, her brows. You decide if you're the right fit.

It is best to have the consultation about a week or two prior to the procedure so that the client is able to best prepare her skin as per the Before Care Instructions you will provide her with.

The first, and I believe, the most important thing to do is get their medical history. Certain conditions can be worked around while others make it impossible. It is important to know which are which. For example, did you know that a thyroid condition can affect the way the pigment colors heal, making them less predictable?

The following conditions can't/shouldn't be worked on:

- Skin that keloids
- Sunburned skin
- Persons on Chemotherapy
- Pregnant or breastfeeding
- HIV or hepatitis
- Eczema or psoriasis on the brows
- Moles or birthmarks on the brows
- An open wound

I always have the client bring me pictures of eyebrows she likes. I have her try to look at faces that resemble hers to keep her realistic about what will suit her best and to get an idea of what kind of eyebrows she sees for herself (I know there are men who microblade their eyebrows, but since 99% will be women and for the sake of ease,

I will refer to the client as female for the rest of this book. Sorry guys). Now, it's time to look at different eyebrows and to pick one that you both feel will be right for her.

It is important to take the shape of the face into consideration. As a general rule, a long face will do better with a straighter brow to give the illusion of a shorter face.

- **Oval faces** do well with softly angled brows
- **Square faces** need soft curves to soften their sharp angles
- **Heart-shaped faces** do well with low rounded arches which create a natural look while a high arch brow will elongate a short face.
- **Round faces** do well with high arches which give the illusion of elongating the face while adding angles as well.
- **Diamond-shaped faces** do well with medium high soft curves

Bringing the brows too close together will create a masculine and authoritative look. This may be good for the male clientele. Spacing them a little further apart will make eyes that are too close together seem less so.

For more detailed information on the right eyebrow shapes, visit: www.eyebrowz.com.

It's important that you both come to an agreement on which brows you will be giving her at the consultation for 2 reasons:

1) Your client has time to think about the shape and change her mind if need be.

2) In case you both are unable to come to an agreement on the proper shape for her face as you see it.

Let's say she wants something that you know will not suit her and you don't want your reputation to get damaged by putting out work that you know is subpar. It is better to make the decision to go your separate ways at the consultation, than on the day of the appointment where you have already booked out 2 hours or more of your time.

So now you've agreed on the shape of the brow and you've determined that she has the right skin type. You've talked about the color and decided on the right one. At this point, you can do a patch test behind her ear, if you so choose. Some do, some don't, the choice is between you and your client. Unless it is a requirement by your insurance company, you are not required to give one. Having said that, it is always a good idea. It is better for her to have a small reaction behind her ears, than two huge ones above her eyes. If you do chose to give a patch test, one little scratch with pigment that is as light as possible behind her ear is all it takes. Remember not to apply any pressure as the skin back there is really thin. Once that's done, you go over each of them before care instructions with her and give her a copy for her to take. You explain to her what the microblading process is; the importance of proper after-care and what to expect from the healing process. You take a non-refundable deposit and book her an appointment.

CHAPTER 3
CLIENT FORMS

Medical History Form
Before Care Instructions
Possible Risks & Hazards Form
Tattoo Consent Form
Pigment Lightening Release Form
Pigment Lightening After-Care Form
Model Photo Release Form
After-Care Forms

CORINNE ASCH

Client Medical History Form

Date_____ Birthdate_____

Name_____

Address_____

Phone_____ Email_____

Emergency Contact Person_____ Phone_____

Do you have or previously had any of the following: (Cirlce YES or No)

YES NO History of MRSA
YES NO Botox (Last treatment_____)
YES NO Diabetes
YES NO Hepatitis A B C D
YES NO Forehead/Brow Lift
YES NO Easy Bleeding
YES NO Facelift
YES NO Alcoholism
YES NO Abnormal Heart Condition
YES NO Take medication before dental work
YES NO Chemical Peel (Last Treatment_____)
YES NO Pregnant now – Breastfeeding now
YES NO Brow Lash Tinting
YES NO Autoimmune disorder
YES NO Oily Skin
YES NO Cancer (Year_____)
YES NO Accutane or acne treatment
YES NO Chemotherapy/ Radiation
YES NO Tan by booth or salon
YES NO Tumors/ Growth/ Cysts
YES NO Difficulty numbing with dental work
YES NO Taking blood thinners such as: Aspirin, Ibuprofen, Alcohol, Coumadin etc
YES NO Allergic reaction to any medications such as Lidocaine, Tetracaine, Epinephrine, Dermacaine, Benzyl Alcohol, Carbopol, Lecithin, Propylene Glycol, Vitamin E Acetate, etc_____
YES NO Allergies to metals, food, etc_____
YES NO Any diseases or disorders not listed_____
YES NO Do you use skin care products containing Retin-A, Glycolic Acid, or Alpha Hydroxyl?
Please list any medications you are taking_____

I agree that all the above information is true and accurate to the best of my knowledge

Signed_____ Date_____

Before Care

- Do not work out on the day of the procedure

- Do not drink too much coffee on the day of the procedure

- Do not tan (no sun) for one week prior to the procedure

- Do not take aspirin, niacin, vitamin E or ibuprofen 24 hours before procedure

- No alcohol the night prior or on the day of the procedure

- Any waxing or tinting of the brows should be done 3 days prior

- No botox for 4 weeks prior to the procedure

- It is best to do a scrub 3 days prior to the procedure

- Stop using any Retin-A or AHA products for 2 weeks prior to the procedure

- No lasers or chemical peels for 1 month prior to the procedure

- No microdermabrasion or dermaplaning for 2 weeks prior

CORINNE ASCH

Possible Risks, Hazards, or Complications

- **Pain:** There can be pain even after the topical anesthetic has been used. Anesthetics work better on some people than on others.

- **Infection:** Infection is very unusual. The areas treated must be kept clean, and only freshly cleaned hands should touch the areas. See "After Care" sheet for instruction on care.

- **Uneven Pigmentation:** This can result from poor healing, infection, bleeding, or many other causes. Your follow-up appointment will likely correct any uneven appearance.

- **Asymmetry:** Every effort will be made to avoid asymmetry, but out faces our not symmetrical so adjustments may be needed during the follow-up session to correct any unevenness.

- **Excessive Swelling or Bruising**: Some people bruise or swell more than others. Ice packs may help reduce the swelling. The swelling or bruising typically disappears in 1-5 days. Some people don't bruise or swell at all.

- **Anesthetics:** Topical anesthetics are used to numb the area to be tattooed. Lidocaine, Prilocaine, Benzocaine, Tetracaine, and/or Epinephrine cream and/or liquid are used. If you are allergic to any of these, please inform me now.

- **MRI:** Because pigments used in Permanent Cosmetic procedures contain inert oxides, a low level magnet may be required if you need to be scanned by an MRI machine. You must inform your MRI Technician of any tattoos or permanent cosmetics.

The alternative to these possibilities is to use traditional cosmetic and NOT undergo the Semi-Permanent Eyebrow procedure.

Consent and release for procedures performed:

Signed_____Date_____

THE MICROBLADING BIBLE

Tattoo Consent Form

I _____ (Client) hereby consent to and authorize

_____ (tattoo artist) to perform the following procedure:

_____

I have voluntarily elected to undergo this treatment/procedure after the nature and purpose of this treatment has been explained to me, along with the risks and hazards involved _____(initials).

Although it is impossible to list every potential risk and complication, I have been informed of possible benefits, risks, and complications. I also recognize there are no guaranteed results and that independent results are dependent upon age, skin condition, and lifestyle. _____(initials)

I understand that this is a 2 and sometimes 3-step process and I will be required to return no later than 60 days after initial procedure for further treatments to obtain the expected results. Anytime past the 60-day period will require payment. _____(initials)

I have read and understand the post-treatment home care instructions. I understand how important it is to follow all instructions given to me for post-treatment care. _____(initials)

I have also, to the best of my knowledge, given an accurate account of my medical history, including all known allergies or prescription drugs or products I am currently ingesting or using topically. _____

I acknowledge that the proposed procedure involves risks inherent in the procedure, and have possibilities of complications during and/or following the procedure such as: infection, poor color retention and hyper-pigmentation _____(initials)

I have read and fully understand this agreement and all information detailed above. I understand the procedure and accept the risks. All of my questions have been answered to my satisfaction and I consent to the terms of this agreement. I do not hold the esthetician, whose signature appears below, responsible for any of my conditions that were present, but not disclosed at the time of this skin care procedure, which may be affected by the treatment performed today.

_____
Client Name (printed)

_____Date_____
Client Name (signature)

_____Date_____
Technician/Tattoo Artist

THE MICROBLADING BIBLE

CONSENT FOR PIGMENT LIGHTENING

Name (Please Print)
_____

The nature and method of the proposed pigment lightening procedure has been explained to me, including risks or possibility of complications during or following its performance. I understand there may be a certain amount of discomfort or pain associated with the procedure and that the other adverse side effects may include: minor and temporary bleeding, bruising, redness or other discoloration and swelling. Secondary infection in the area of the procedure may occur. However, if properly cared for, this is rare. _____ (initials)

I understand that several treatments may be needed in order to attempt to achieve my desired results. _____(initials)

I understand that the previous unwanted pigment may not be successfully lightened to the point that it can no longer be seen. Scarring as hyper-pigmentation or hypo-pigmentation, or other damage to the skin may occur during this process and may be permanent. I will not hold my technician and /or the distributor of tattoo removal products used in this attempted pigment removal liable for any damages that may occur to my person. _____(initials)

Which of the following best describes your skin type? (please circle one number)

      I. Always burns, never tans
     II. Always burns, sometimes tans
    III. Sometimes burns, always tans
    IV. Rarely burns, always tans
     V. Brown, moderately pigmented skin
    VI. Black skin

For skin types V and VI and saline removals only:
I understand that I am at a higher risk for hyper-pigmentation and hypo-pigmentation than other skin types. I agree to the risks involved. _____(initials)

I understand that lightening tattoo pigment is difficult, if even possible, and that there are no guarantees with this procedure. As a result, I will not hold my technician or this establishment responsible for any resultant failure to lighten the unwanted pigment _____(initials)

I agree to submit to before and after photographs, and give my permission to use such photographs for publication and/or teaching purposes. _____(initials)

I agree to follow all after-care instructions provided by my technician. _____(initials)

I have been duly informed of the risks, possible complications and consequences as listed above. _____(initials)

I understand all information listed above, have had my questions answered, and agree to all conditions and provisions of this document as evidenced by my signature below. I accept the risks for having this procedure done. _____(initials)

_____
Client Name (please print)

_____Date_____
Client Signature

_____Date_____
Technician/Tattoo Artist

THE MICROBLADING BIBLE

MODEL PHOTO RELEASE FORM
(Your company name)

I hereby give permission to

_____

tattoo artist

to use my photographic likeness in all forms and media for advertising, exposition displays, trade, teaching materials and any other lawful purposes.

Print Name: _____

Signature: _____ Date _____

After Care Instructions

1. Clean the treatment area on the night of procedure and daily thereafter. Apply a thin layer of after-care balm, grapeseed or coconut oil to the treatment area twice daily (once if you have oily skin), being careful not to over saturate. A thin layer is all you need.

2. Besides gently cleansing the procedure area daily, keep water off of your brows for the next 5 days. That includes sweating, saunas and hot showers.

3. Do not use any face creams, exfoliators, or harsh cleansers on your brows during the healing process.

4. Normal activity can be resumed immediately, but no heavy exercise such as aerobic dancing, weight lifting, swimming, etc. for the next 10 days.

5. Your procedure will begin to oxidize immediately. This causes the pigment to become darker. Do not be alarmed, this dark color will fade during the next few days.

6. Do not pick any scabs or dry areas that may form during the healing process. This may cause you to lose color or damage your skin. Instead, apply some of the after-care your technician gave you after the procedure.

7. Other fading or loss of pigment may occur. Some flaking off of the pigment is normal on some skin types; the pigment may sometimes, disappear only to re-appear a few days or weeks later. Any pigment loss will be recovered at touch up.

Lightening/Removal Client After-Care

It is critical to follow all aftercare instructions to prevent complications, scarring and to achieve optimum results. Please read the following carefully.

1. KEEP THE AREA CLEAN and open to the air. Do not cover with a Band-Aid or anything else, leave open to air. Air/oxygen provides good and faster healing. You should not be touching the area at all, but if you find yourself needing to, please make sure your hands are exceptionally clean.

2. DO NOT SOAK the treated area in water. You can shower as normal but keep the area out of the shower spray the best you can and do not let the area stay wet for more than a few minutes.

3. NO BATHING, SWIMMING, SAUNAS, HOT TOBS, TANNING, OR INTENSE EXERCISE.

4. DO NOT disrupt the scabbing process (i.e. no picking, scratching, etc.) All scabbing needs to fall off naturally. If you force or pick a scab off you will disrupt the process and possibly cause scarring.

5. TREAT AREA WITH TLC. DO NOT DO ANYTHING AT ALL THAT COULD CAUSE ISSUE OR PROBLEMS TO THE TREATED AREA. IF YOU ARE NOT SURE OR HAVE ANY QUESTIONS, PLEASE CALL OR EMAIL

6. ONCE ALL SCABBING HAS NATURALLY FALLEN OFF, apply one drop of Vitamin E Oil 4 to 6 times throughout the day for a minimum of 4 weeks, or until next lightening session. DO NOT start applying the Vitamin E oil UNTIL all scabbing has completely fallen off. It is our goal to keep the area as dry as possible until all scabs have naturally fallen off.

- It is important to the process and integrity of the skin that 8 full weeks of healing take place before another lightening session can be done. No exceptions

- Lightening and/or removing unwanted pigment is a long process and patience is required. This is true whether you are choosing a lightening product service or laser treatement. Please be patient and give the process a fair chance to work. Expect visible and wanted results in 3 to 6 sessions. How many sessions needed will depend on how saturated the pigment is, how deep it was implanted and how much needs to be removed for the desired result. In many cases, only a percentage of the density needs to be lightened/removed and then we can continue the correction process by color correcting. In cases where we have pigment misplaced or in an unwanted area, color correcting will not be an option and removing as much of the pigment as possible will be our ultimate goal.

- Results cannot be foreseen, predicted or guaranteed.

CHAPTER 4
THE IMPORTANCE OF PROPER STERILIZATION

Sterilization is a big topic and varies from state to state and country to country. It is very important to get familiar with the laws in your area. Beyond that and for the protection of your client and yourself there are precautions you must take no matter what.

One teacher told me to handle each client as though they have HIV. I thought that was sage advice.

Following are the standard legal requirements. Be sure to check your local laws regarding tattooing and sterilization.

General Requirements:

- Possess a current Infection Prevention Control Plan
- Facility is clean, free of insects and rodents and has walls, floors and ceilings that are smooth, washable and free of holes.
- All practitioners are registered with certificates posted.
- A contract for removal of all sharps waste
- Waste containers with liners in proceure area and decontamination area.
- Properly labeled sharps containers that are within arms reach of the practioners in the procedure and decontamination areas.

Procedure Areas:

- Equipped with adequate lighting
- Equipped with hand washing sink with hot and cold running water, liquid soap, and single use towels in a touchless dispenser.

Decontamination Areas:
(Not required if only disposable, single-use, and pre-sterilized instruments are used)

  o Separated from procedure areas by at least 5 feet or by a cleanable barrier

- Equipped with a sink with hot and cold running water for cleaning and disinfecting equipment
- Only equipment manufactured for sterilization of medical instruments may be used
- Upon initial installation, after repair, and at least monthly, the sterilization unit must be tested using a commercial biological indicator monitoring system.

1. An autoclave is a must for anything that you will re-use.

2. Instruments or other reusable items shall be washed, disinfected, packaged, and sterilized after each procedure. Packages shall contain either an integrator or process indicator and shall be labeled with name of instrument, date and initials.

3. Used, reusable instruments are to be stored in liquid until cleaned and sterilized. An instrument or reusable item that does not come into contact with non-intact skin shall be washed, scrubbed and decontaminated after each procedure.

4. Your autoclave will need to be spore tested once a month. Test results shall be recorded in a log.

5. The decontamination/sterilization area must be separate from the procedure area and supplied with a sink with hot and cold running water, containerized liquid soap, and paper towels in a wall-mounted dispenser that is readily accessible to the practitioner. You'll need a line waste container and sharps containers.

6. A body art facility lacking a cleaning room and sterilization equipment shall use only disposable, single-use, pre sterilized instruments and maintain records of purchase, use, procedures (include name of practitioner and client and procedure date). Keep records for at least 90 days.

7. Sharps containers must be within arm's reach, labeled and disposed of by the approved method. Documentation of proper disposal available and maintained for 3 years. Sharps waste includes, needles and needle bars, and hand tools if needle is part of unit.

8. No food, drink, tobacco product, or personal effects are permitted in the procedure area.

9. Practitioner shall wash hands in approved manner before procedure and when soiled.

10. Hand washing sink in the procedure area is supplied, has potable warm water and is accessible.

11. The practitioner shall use appropriate personal protective equipment including gloves, aprons, hair net, and mouth cover. Gloves shall be worn throughout and if removed, hand hygiene shall be performed.

12. Procedure shall not be performed while there is another client in the procedure room.

13. Client must be at least 18 years of age unless parent is present.

14. Skin shall be washed before being shaved. Immediately before performing the microblading procedure, the skin shall be prepared with an antiseptic solution, antimicrobial or microbicide.

15. Practitioner shall clean and decontaminate the area, solid surfaces and objects that have come in contact with client and the materials used during procedure, including chairs, armrests, table countertops and trays before and after procedure.

16. Barrier film is to be used on tattooing machine (body, clip, cord, etc.)

17. Products (stencils, marking agents, inks and soaps) applied to skin are single use, dispensed aseptically and/or disinfected for reuse.

18. Clean and/or sterilized instruments and equipment shall be protected during storage in appropriate, intact containers. If sterile packs become compromised, items shall be reprocessed before use.

19. Cross-contamination is avoided during all phases of procedure, including but not limited to set up, the procedure itself and tear down. Wastes generated are discarded immediately after use. The practitioner glove use limits potential cross contamination events.

20. Facility must be separate from any residential areas used for sleeping, bathing, or meal preparation and shall not share an entrance or toilet facility with residence. Procedure area is seperated from salon activities by a wall or a floor to ceiling partition and be separate from all business not related to body art. Mobile body art facilities shall be used only for the purposes of performing body art and body art procedures performed at a mobile facility shall be done only from an approved mobile facility. No body art procedure shall be performed outside of the enclosed mobile facility.

21. Facility shall have floors, walls and ceilings that are smooth, non-absorbent, free of open holes, washable, free of insect and rodent infestation and be equipped with adequate light and ventilation.

22. Procedure area, surfaces, chairs, armrests, etc. shall be in good condition and shall be disinfected.

23. Certificate of Registration and Health Permit shall be posted in a conspicuous place. Owner of the agency shall notify the LEA in writing within 30 days of practitioner changes and shall not allow

a practitioner to work without being registered as a practitioner. The practitioner must be a registered body art practitioner and shall only perform body art from a permitted body art facility.

24. Operation and Employee Training Records shall be present and available upon inspection. Infection Prevention and Control Plan is maintained, followed and updated.

25. Practitioner has current hepatitis B vaccination/applicable booster, can demonstrate immunity or has complied with current federal OSHA hepatitis B vaccination declination requirements.

26. Practitioner shall provide evidence of completion of approved Blood borne Pathogen Training.

27. Toilet facilities must be adequate per state, local or other laws, codes or ordinances. Restroom shall be supplied with permanently plumbed sink, supplied with hot/cold running water, containerized liquid soap, and single use paper towels dispensed from a wall-mounted, touchless dispenser. Approved restroom facilities must be within 200 ft. of mobile art facilities.

28. A person shall not perform body art if he or she is not registered. Registration shall be renewed annually. A body art facility shall have a valid health permit or be subject to penalties and/or closure.

29. Instruments found to be unsafe, used in an unapproved manner or used in an unapproved location, may be impounded by enforcement officers.

30. If an imminent health hazard is found, the enforcement officer may order the practitioner to cease operation if the hazard is not corrected. If the hazard affects the entire body art facility, then the entire facility may be closed immediately. If a person who does not possess a valid practitioner registration is allowed to work, the LEA

may suspend or revoke the facility's permit. A certificate of registration or a health permit may be suspended by a local enforcement agency for a violation of this chapter.

Blood Borne Pathogens

Blood borne pathogens are infectious microorganisms in human blood that can cause disease in humans. These pathogens include, but are not limited to, hepatitis B (HBV), hepatitis C (HCV) and human immunodeficiency virus (HIV). Needle stick and other sharps-related injuries may expose workers to blood borne pathogens. Workers in many occupations, including first responders, housekeeping personnel in some industries, nurses and other healthcare personnel, may all be at risk for exposure to blood borne pathogens.

How are blood borne pathogens and infections spread?

For disease to be spread, it requires that all of the following conditions be present:

- An adequate number of pathogens, or disease-causing organisms.
- A reservoir or source that allows the pathogen to survive and multiply (e.g. blood).
- A mode of transmission from the source to the host.
- An entrance through which the pathogen may enter the host.
- A susceptible host (i.e., one who is not immune).
- Effective infection control strategies prevent disease transmission by interrupting one or more links in the chain of infection.
- Bodily fluids, especially those visibly contaminated with blood,

have the potential to transmit disease. When a contaminated sharp object cuts or punctures the skin. (Parenteral examples: needle stick, illegal drug usage, cut from broken glass, bite) When an infected body fluid gets into an open cut or mucous membrane (inside eyes, mouth, ears or nose) When a contaminated object touches inflamed skin, acne, or skin abrasion.

Direct contact- occurs when microorganisms are transferred from one infected person directly to another person. For example, infected blood from one person enters a care giver's body through an open cut.

Indirect contact- involves the transfer of an infectious agent through a contaminated object or person. For example, when a caregiver doesn't wash hands in between caring for someone with infected body fluids and other patients. For example, parenteral contact with a needle stick.

Airborne transmission- occurs when droplets or small particles contain infectious agents that remain effective over time and distance in the air. Tuberculosis is a common disease spread this way. Blood borne pathogens are not typically spread this way.

Clients must provide "Informed Consent"

To provide informed consent, client must read an informed consent form that includes a description of the procedure, a description of what to expect after the procedure, a statement regarding the permanent nature of body art (in the case of microblading, the brow of this statement would be the length of time the pigment will last); a notice that tattoo inks, dyes and pigments have not been approved by the Federal Food and Drug Administration and the health consequences of using these products are unknown.

The informed consent form should also include a client health questionnaire to determine if the client is pregnant, has a history of herpes infections at the procedure site, diabetes, allergic reaction to latex or antibiotics, hemophilia or other bleeding disorder, cardiac valve disease, has a history of medication use, including prescribed antibiotics prior to dental or surgical procedures or has other risk factors for blood borne pathogen exposure. The client must also provide post-procedure instructions.

What can be done to control exposure to blood borne pathogens?

In order to reduce or eliminate the hazards of occupational exposure to blood borne pathogens, an employer must implement an exposure control plan for the worksite with details on employee protection measures. The plan must also describe how an employer will use engineering and work practice controls, personal protective clothing and equipment, employee training, medical surveillance, hepatitis-B vaccinations, and other provisions as required by OSHA's Blood Borne Pathogens Standard.

If you are stuck by a needle or other sharp object or get blood in your eyes, nose, mouth, or on broken skin, immediately flood the exposed area with water and clean any wound with soap and water or a skin disinfectant. Report this immediately to your employer and seek immediate medical attention.

Requirements for Safe Performance of Body Art

- Wash and dry hands before beginning a procedure

- Put on a clean apron, bib, or lap pad and personal protective equipment appropriate to the task.

- Put on clean, unused, disposable exam gloves just prior to the procedure and wear the gloves throughout the procedure. Wash hands and change gloves if contact occurs with surfaces other than the client's skin or instruments used in the procedure or if glove is punctured or torn.

- Apply antiseptic, antimicrobial, or microbicide to the client's skin immediately prior to the procedure.

- Use a single-use razor to shave client and dispose of the razor in the Sharps container.

- Only single-use needles and needle bars may be used and must be disposed of in the Sharps container.

- Any part of a tattooing machine that may be touched by a practitioner during the procedure shall be covered with a disposable plastic sheath that is discarded upon completion of the procedure.

- Instruments other than the needles and needle bars that contact skin must be either be single use or be washed, disinfected, packaged, and sterilized after each procedure.

- Only commercially manufactured inks, dyes, and pigments may be used and must be dispensed in a manner to prevent contamination of the storage container and remaining contents.

- After the procedure, wash and disinfect instruments and decontaminate the workstation and procedure area.

- No food, drink, tobacco product, or personal effects are permitted in the procedure area.

- Animals, with the exception of service animals, are not permitted in the procedure area or decontamination- sterilization area.

Decontamination and Sterilization Requirements

* Each instrument peel-packs must have an appropriate indicator.

* Each sterilization load shall be monitored with a Class V integrator.

* Sterilization units are to be loaded, operated, decontaminated, and maintained according to manufacturer specifications.

* A written log of each sterilization cycle including date, contents, exposure time, temperature and the results of the Class V integrator must be retained on site for two years.

* Sterilization packs must be inspected prior to storage and again prior to use.

Standard Precautions

Treat all body fluids from every person as potentially infectious. Follow the recommendations in the employer's Blood Borne Pathogens Exposure Control Plan

An employer's Blood Borne Pathogens Exposure Control Plan should include:

* Various levels of risk of employees that may have occupational exposure
* Training requirements
* Work practice controls
* Engineering controls
* Procedure for an exposure incident

Use personal protective equipment

- Gloves, CPR shields, masks, gowns, eye protection

- Know where PPE is at your workplace

- Know what PPE is available and how to use it

- Make sure first-aid kits and emergency supplies include disposable gloves and CPR face shields or rescue masks

How to Reduce Your Risk

* Do not eat, drink, smoke, apply cosmetics or handle contact lenses in areas where there is the possibility of exposure to BBP.

* When emptying trash containers, do not use your hands to compress the trash in the bag. Lift and carry the trash bag away from your body.

* Keep contaminated laundry separate from other laundry. Bag potentially contaminated laundry where it is used.

* Use leak-proof bags for wet laundry. Transport in properly labeled bags.
* The Needle stick Prevention Act requires appropriate, commercially available, and effectively safer medical devices designed to eliminate or minimize occupational exposure.

* Needles and other sharps must be discarded in rigid, leak-proof, puncture-resistant containers.

* Do not bend, shear, break or recap needles.

* If you must recap, use the one-handed method.

Hazardous Disposal

Liquid or semi-liquid blood or other potentially infectious materials (OPIM).

Contaminated items that would release blood or other potentially infectious materials in a liquid or semi-liquid state if compressed.

Dispose of in a properly labeled biohazard container: either a red bag or container labeled in orange or orange-red with the Bio-Hazard symbol.

Properly labeled and bundled waste needs to be handled according to your facility's disposal procedures.

Clean-up Procedure

* Use a solution of 1part household bleach mixed with 9 parts water (a 1:10 solution).

* Other commercial disinfectants registered with the EPA as effective against HIV/HBV may be used. Check the label.

* Use Personal Protective Equipment.

* If a Body Fluid Spill Kit is available, use according to manufacturer's directions.

* First, put on Personal Protective Equipment.

* Remove visible material with absorbent towels.

* If any sharp object or broken glass is visible, remove wi   ngs or dust pan and place in a rigid sealable container. Nev hands.

* Spray disinfectant on contaminated area and let it stand for several minutes.

* Once the area has been disinfected, dry area with absorbent towels and dispose of towels in regular trash.

Proper Glove Removal

* Grip one glove near the cuff and peel it down until it comes off inside out. Cup it in the palm of your gloved hand.

* Place two fingers of your bare hand inside the cuff of the remaining glove.

* Peel that glove down so that it also comes off inside out and over the first glove.

* Properly dispose of the gloves.

* Remember, only touch glove to glove and skin to skin.

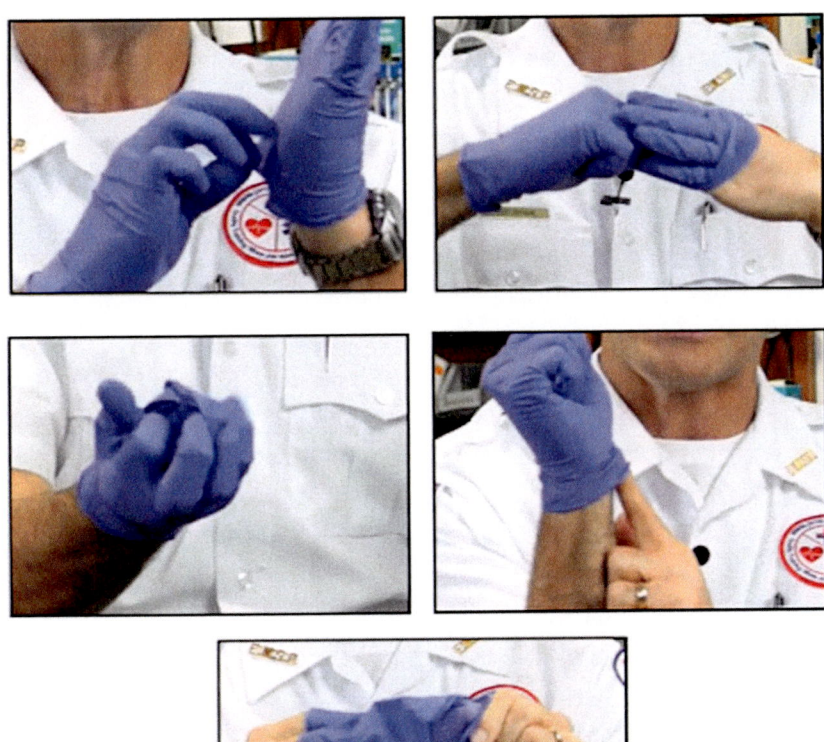

Exposure Incident

* An exposure incident is defined as a specific mucous membrane, broken skin, or puncture contact with blood or OPIM that results from the performance of an employee's duties.

* If you think you've been exposed, decontaminate, report to supervisor, and seek medical treatment. An immediate confidential medical evaluation and follow-up needs to be conducted by a physician.

* Complete forms as soon as possible after incident. Don't delay medical treatment to fill out paperwork. Forms and continued action will proceed according to employer's policies and procedures.

Sterile Water Use in Tattooing

The use of non-sterile water in tattooing activities has been associated with a number of water-borne skin infections caused by bacteria such as Legionella, Pseudomonas and Mycobacteria. These infections can result in severe illness and when left untreated, they may be fatal. Even mild infections can commonly result in skin scarring and damage to the tattoo. Water that is not sterile, including tap, bottled, "spring", reverse osmosis filtered, and distilled water, may not be safe to cleanse the skin, rinse needles and to dilute inks that are injected into the skin.

The Center for Disease Control and Prevention recommend the use of sterile water when tattooing. Another safe option is the use of sterile saline solution. While there are no current regulations that require this practice, artists concerned with the health and safety of their customers have incorporated the use of sterile water or sterile saline for ink dilution, rinsing of needles, and rinsing of skin during their tattoo procedures.

The use of sterile water or sterile saline solution can help protect your customers from water-borne skin infections that can hurt their health and damage the body art you created for them.

CHAPTER 5
GETTING TO KNOW THE FITZPATRICKS

The Fitzpatrick Scale was developed in 1975 by Dr. Thomas Fitzpatrick, a Harvard University dermatologist. Our society has changed quite a bit since then. One of the challenges of skin typing is that we are becoming increasingly multi-racial and multi-ethnic. Therefore, the color of our skin alone cannot determine reactivity to products.

For example, we typically associate sensitive skin with very fair, thin, delicate skin. But black skin can be sensitive too. What happens to skin if it is multi-racial? It certainly makes it more challenging to correctly predict how skin will respond. Nevertheless, the Fitzpatrick Scale is still a useful tool for predicting how the skin will react to different pigments. The color of your skin is correlated with the amount of melanin in your skin. That can be vital information when figuring out how much modifier you will need to create the color you want.

The scale is divided into six different skin types. Check out the different indicators for each type to determine which category your skin falls into.

The Fitzpatrick Scale

Type 1	Type 2	Type 3	Type 4	Type 5	Type 6
Light, Pale White	White, Fair	Medium, White to Olive	Olive, Moderate Brown	Brown, Dark Brown	Black, Very dark Brown to Black
Always burns. Never tans	Usually Burns. Tans with difficulty	Sometimes mild burns, gradually tans to Olive	Rarely burns. Tans with ease to a Moderate Brown	Very rarely burns. Tans very easily	Never burns. Tans Very easily. Deeply Pigmented

Type 1: Type 1 skin types have the least amount of melanin in the skin. You only burn and never tan. You have very pale skin with no ⟨...⟩nes, and you have red or blond hair. You sometimes ⟨...⟩nd have blue or green eyes.

Type 2: Type 2 skin types are also very pale skinned with very little melanin; you only burn and never tan. You can sometimes have pink undertones and can have dark hair, although you almost always have blond or light brown hair. Your eye color ranges from light blue to dark green and hazel.

Type 3: As a type 3 skin type, you may burn at the beginning of the summer, but tan easily afterwards. Your medium to olive skin tone has more melanin than the previous 2 types. Your eyes are sometimes dark hazel, but mostly dark brown. Your hair is brown.

Type 4: Your medium-brown skin tans easily and rarely burns. You have dark hair and eyes.

Type 5: Type 5 skin tans very easily and seldom burns. Dark hair, dark eyes and dark skin are your characteristics.

Type 6: As the darkest skin type, you almost never burn and tan very easily. Your eyes are almost always dark and your hair is always dark.

What is skin undertone?

Your skin's undertone is not about how light or dark your skin is, rather it is the color that comes through from underneath the skin's surface to affect the overall tonal quality. Whether you have light, medium or dark skin, your skin can have warm, cool, or neutral undertones. So how do you determine a client's undertones?

Basically, this sums it up:

* Cool: Hints of bluish, pink or a ruddy complexion.
* Warm: Skin skews yellow, sallow, peachy or golden.

* Neutral: Has no obvious overtones of pink or sallow skin, but rather the skin's natural color is more evident.

1. Check Your Veins
Push your sleeves up right now and look at the veins on the inside of your wrist. Are they blue or green? If they look more blue, you likely have cool undertones. If the veins look greenish, you're warm. It's worth noting, warm girls, that your veins aren't actually green—they look it because you're seeing them through yellow-toned skin (yellow + blue = green.)

2. Eye and Hair Color
Your natural eye and hair colors can help figure out your coloring. Customarily, cool people have eyes that are blue, gray, or green and have blond, brown, or black hair with blue, silver, violet and ash undertones. Conversely, warm-toned women usually have brown, amber, or hazel eyes with strawberry blond, red, brown, or black hair. Their hair tends to have gold, red, orange, or yellow undertones.

3. The Sun's Effects.
As the Fitzpatrick scale suggests, when you're out in the sun, does your skin turn a golden-brown, or does it burn and turn pink first? If you fit into the former category, you're warm-toned, while cool tones tend to burn (fair-skinned cool girls will simply burn, while medium-skinned cool-toned girls will burn then tan).

4. The White Cloth Test
Put a white cloth next to your bare face and observe what cast your skin takes on. Skin with warm undertones will appear yellowish, while skin with cool undertones will seem blueish or pinkish. If your test results are coming out mixed, you may, in fact have neutral undertones.

5. Do You Blush Easily?
If so, then you're on the cool side.

6. Who Do You Identify With?

Think celebrities. Scarlett Johansson, Anne Hathaway, Lucy Liu, Demi Moore, Courtney Cox, Sandra Bullock, Jennifer Hudson, and Amanda Seyfried have cool undertones.

Nicole Kidman, Jennifer Lopez, Beyoncé, Jessica Alba, Kate Hudson, Diane Sawyer, and Kim Kardashian have warm undertones.

CHAPTER 6
UNDERSTANDING PIGMENTS

It would be nice if the color you choose is the color you end up with, but it also makes sense that the pigment or the color of the skin you're working on makes a contribution to the chosen color/s. Knowing your colors and modifiers and then learning how to use them on which skin tone is a whole class in itself.

If you use Li pigment, and many do, Teryn Darling and Mary Ritcherson give an excellent online course on color theory. Whatever line you decide to use, make sure they give strong educational support.

When selecting a pigment for your client, you must use your experience and fast forward in your mind the effect the client's skin tone will have in relationship with the pigment you are putting in the skin.

Pigment color + skin tone = outcome color

The obvious question regarding pigments is why couldn't we have colors that heal the same color as when it's in the bottle, and the reason is, because we all have different skin undertones that effect the colors we use. This is why it's important to know your Fitzpatrick scale and to get your color education from whichever line of pigments you choose.

Pigments will almost always heal on the cool side, some more than others.

How the colors fade when the time comes, also has everything to do with the quality of the pigments you use. There are a lot of new companies popping up every month. Some will be good, most will not. Be very careful in choosing your line of pigments. Remember, you will be implanting these pigments into people's skin. Cheaper or low quality pigments can cause all kinds of problems, the worst of them could be an allergic reaction to some of the ingredients in the pigment. Once you buy a whole line of pigments, it is expensive to switch to another line. Be careful when choosing your line of pigments. Making sure of the line of pigment used and how much training and support you will get, is one of the questions you ask your prospective trainer.

You will want to get to know your pigments and modifiers really well before you get started. Try to err on the side of too light, when starting out, it's much easier to fix than too dark.

With skin types and tones, all rules are general. For example, Fitzpatrick skin types I & II are almost always cool (the pink skin is considered cool) and the pigments for these skin types will need to be warmed up with red or orange based modifiers.

How much it will need to be warmed will depend on how cool the skin tone is to begin with. This is where experience becomes your best advisor. If you're not sure, you can take a picture of your client at the consultation and post it on the Facebook microblading boards and you will get lots of help and advice.

The Fitzpatrick skin in the III, IV & V range are usually not as cool and can have yellow, or very often in the middle eastern woman, have purple undertones which can be balanced with green or violet based modifiers. Again, how much modifier you'll need will depend on the intensity of your undertones.

This is where knowing your color wheel becomes helpful in choosing the right modifiers. A clear understanding of color theory is the first step to knowing how to counteract unwanted colors and produce beautiful colors for your clients.

We begin with a 3-part color wheel.

Primary Colors

Secondary Colors

Tertiary Colors

Primary Colors:
Red, yellow and blue

In traditional color theory (used in paint and pigments), primary colors are the 3 pigment colors that cannot be mixed or formed by any combination of other colors. All other colors are derived from these 3 hues.

Secondary Colors:
Green, orange and purple

These are the colors formed by mixing the primary colors.

Tertiary Colors:
Yellow-orange, red-orange, red-purple, blue-purple, blue-green & yellow-green.

These are the colors formed by mixing a primary and a secondary color. That's why the hue is a two-word name, such as blue-green, red-violet, and yellow-orange.

The Color Wheel

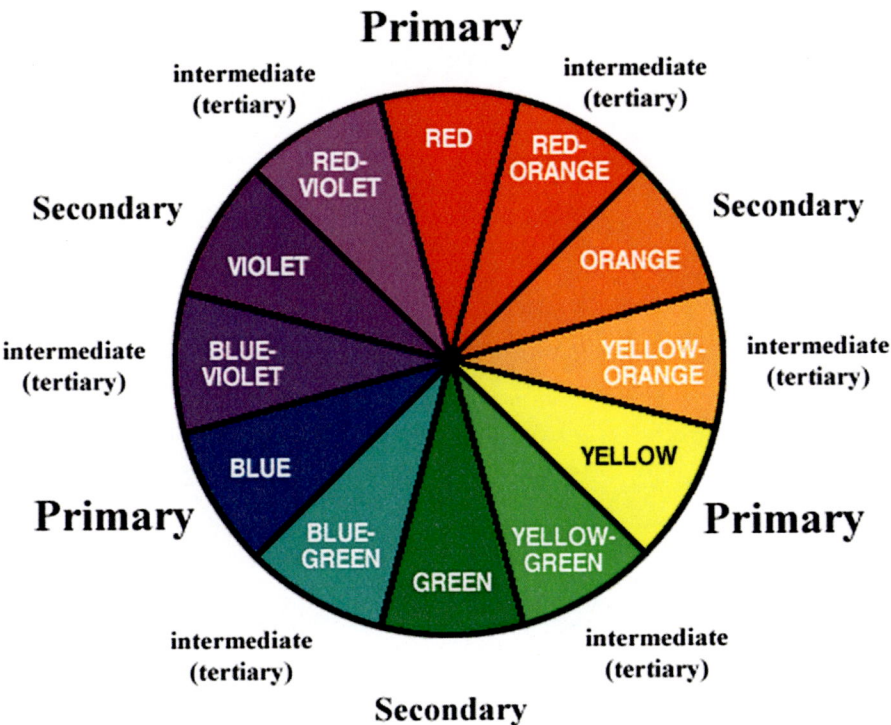

Opposing color scheme

Colors that are opposite on the color wheel will neutralize each other and are the way to counteract unwanted colors (example: red and green cancel each other out) and to create colors you do want (example: adding yellow to your pigment to create a golden tone).

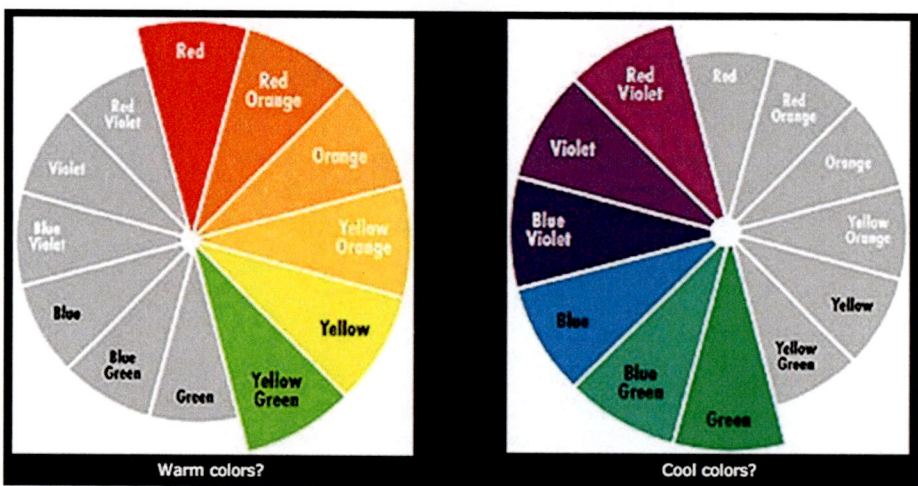

The first step in grasping the concept? Understanding that our skin's surface tone is the color you'd describe yourself as having (ivory, light, medium, tan, dark, etc.). Your skin's undertone is the color underneath the surface. You can have the same skin color as someone, but a different undertone, which are broken down like this:

- Cool (pink, red or bluish undertones)
- Warm (yellow, peachy, golden undertones)
- Neutral (a mix of warm and cool undertones)

One big misconception: That pale girls can't be warm-toned. In fact, many fair-skinned women have warm undertones (Nicole Kidman is one of them!) and dark-skinned women have cool tones (supermodel Alek Wek is a cool tone).

Warm and cool colors

The color circle can be divided into warm and cool colors. White, black and gray are considered to be neutral.

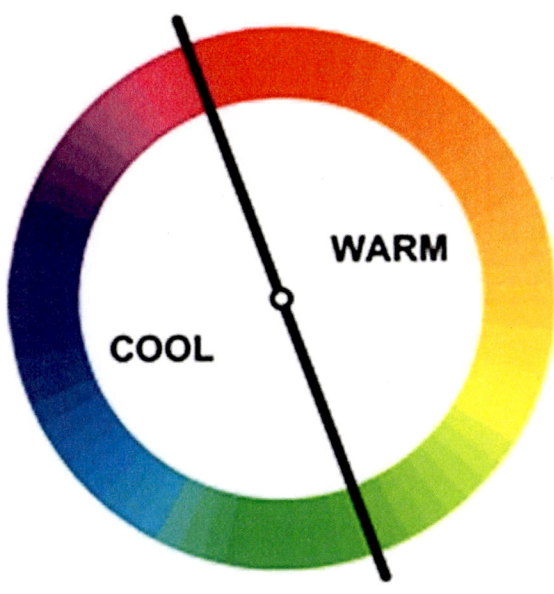

CHAPTER 7
TO NUMB OR NOT TO NUMB

This is the most controversial of all the microblading topics. Whether to numb before the first strokes or not.

The perfectionists say numbing shifts the eyebrow placement and constricts blood-flow which interferes with the ability to read the skin. The opposing view is that keeping the client comfortable with them not twitching or moving during the procedure is what will yield the best results, and, they will tell you they've never had a problem with numbing first.

Both make good points.

Trivia:
Did you know that when your body feels pain, it becomes stressed which in turn makes it pump out more blood?

Studies show that people with red hair are naturally more sensitive to pain and less receptive to skin numbing creams?

Typically, if you choose to numb your client prior to the procedure, it is best to use a numbing cream which is topical and fast acting, but only works on the surface. Anesthesia will leave behind an oily residue, which when left on the skin, will affect the consistency of the ink. This could result in the ink not penetrating deeply enough. This is why it is important to make sure that all anesthetic residue is thoroughly cleaned from the skin before beginning the procedure.

Once the skin is broken, a gel numbing agent will work best. It will soothe from the inside out and is used as a top up anesthetic. This will also reduce trauma and discomfort to your client.

Out of the 4 key numbing agents: Lidocaine, tetracaine, benzocaine and epinephrine, lidocaine is the one you'll find in nearly every tattoo anesthetic product. Over the counter topical anesthetics made in the

U.S. can contain up to 5% lidocaine. The higher the percentage, the more effective the product will be at deadening the nerve endings and making the permanent make-up session more comfortable.

You'll find that many tattoo anesthetic products also contain either tetracaine or benzocaine, if not both. These ingredients are actually nerve blockers, rather than nerve deadeners like lidocaine. They don't entirely prevent nerves from sending pain signals to the brain, but they soften the blow.

Epinephrine is a slightly more controversial ingredient that you'll find in some tattoo topical anesthetics. It's a vasoconstrictor and one of the more powerful over-the-counter topical anesthetic ingredients available.

Vasoconstrictors cause the blood vessels to tighten up, minimize bleeding and swelling during the microblading procedure. Since vasoconstrictors also slow down the rate at which the body absorbs a topical anesthetic cream, spray or gel, they also keep the microblading client comfortable longer. However, too much epinephrine can cause the heart rate to accelerate, so use it sparingly- particularly on clients with high anxiety.

Here is a thorough article I found on numbing creams that explains the ingredients and how and when to use them and which ones.

TATTOO ANESTHETIC OPTIONS

JUL 05, 2015 / BY LAURA ON INFORMATION CENTER TATTOO INFORMATION

Some people say that getting a tattoo is all about the pain--that they feel most alive when tattoo needles are puncturing their skin. There are also many tattoo artists who believe that the pain of getting a tattoo is a core part of the process and shouldn't be downplayed. However, there are plenty of people who desperately want a tattoo, but hesitate because they're concerned about their ability to handle the pain factor.

Fortunately, there's a solution that levels the playing field and makes it so that even those with low pain thresholds can get tattooed more comfortably: tattoo anesthetic sprays, numbing creams and anesthetic gels.

Do tattoo anesthetics really work? If so, how do they work? Is there an ideal combination of tattoo anesthetic products that provides maximum pain relief during the tattooing process? We answer these questions and more and discuss some of the best tattoo anesthetic products on the market in the sections below.

Do Tattoo Anesthetics Really Work?

The short answer to this question is yes, tattoo anesthetic products can be very effective even though they're just topical.

Not all tattoo anesthetics are created equal, though. Ideally, it's best to use a tattoo anesthetic that contains one or more of the following key ingredients, which each have a different impact on the pain signals sent to your brain during the tattooing process: lidocaine, tetracaine, benzocaine, and/or epinephrine.

There are also natural additives that can enhance the power of a topical anesthetic, like menthol, camphor, tea tree oil, and comphrey root, just to name a few.

How Do Tattoo Anesthetic Products Work?

Out of the four key numbing agents listed above, lidocaine is one you'll find in nearly every tattoo anesthetic product. Over-the-counter topical anesthetics made in the U.S. can contain up to 5% lidocaine; the higher the percentage, the more effective the product will be at deadening nerve endings and making the tattooing process more comfortable. It's a key ingredient in minimizing the initial sting of tattoo needles hitting the skin and can prevent clients from flinching so much that they compromise their tattoo designs.

You'll find that many tattoo anesthetic products also contain either tetracaine or benzocaine, if not both. These ingredients are actually nerve blockers, rather than nerve deadeners like lidocaine. They don't entirely prevent nerves from sending pain signals to the brain, but they soften the blow of those pain signals, turning "OH MY GOD" pain into a milder level of discomfort that might elicit an "Ooh!" instead.

Epinephrine is a slightly more controversial ingredient that you'll find in some tattoo topical anesthetics. It's a vasoconstrictor and one of the more powerful over-the-counter topical anesthetic ingredients available. Vasoconstrictors cause the blood vessels to tighten up, minimizing bleeding and swelling during the tattooing process.

Since vasoconstrictors also slow down the rate at which the body absorbs a topical anesthetic cream, spray or gel, they also keep tattoo clients comfortable longer. However, too much epinephrine can cause tachycardia, so use topical anesthetics containing epinephrine sparingly-particularly on clients with high anxiety, since epinephrine can cause anxiety to spike along with a client's heart rate.

CORINNE ASCH

What's the Most Effective Combination of Tattoo Anesthetics?

It takes time for the body to absorb a topical anesthetic until it's fully effective, so when you apply one is somewhat more important than which one(s) you apply. Some tattoo anesthetic options are faster acting than others, making them good "boosters" to apply as secondary layers throughout the tattooing process.

When using a tattoo anesthetic containing epinephrine, you shouldn't have to reapply it as frequently while tattooing to maintain a client's comfort level.

Ideally, clients should apply an initial layer of topical anesthetic cream, spray or gel before they even leave home and head over to your tattoo shop.

If you have a design meeting with a client who's worried about the pain factor, encourage them to take a jar or bottle of a tattoo anesthetic like Tattoo Soothe Cream or Hush anesthetic gel home with them and apply it an hour before coming back in to get tattooed. For optimal results, they should apply a thick layer to the area where they're getting tattooed, and then wrap the area with plastic cling wrap to encourage maximum absorption. If you wait to apply a topical anesthetic in your shop before tattooing someone, the client will need to wait anywhere from 15 to 60 minutes before you can start, in order to get the most benefit from the topical anesthetic applied.

During the skin prep part of the tattooing process, consider washing clients' skin with a product like H2Ocean's Nothing Pain-Relieving Foam Soap or Green Soap enhanced with Bactine to reinforce the effects of any topical anesthetic applied earlier. These antiseptic skin cleansers also contain lidocaine and other numbing agents that will amplify the effects of any topical anesthetic already applied.

If you start tattooing a client with a low pain threshold and find they're still uncomfortable, you can apply a secondary layer of a fast-acting topical anesthetic like Tattoo Soothe topical anesthetic gel, Hush anesthetic spray or Feel Better Now numbing gel. These products are effective within 90 seconds to 5 minutes after application when used as a secondary layer of pain relief, and they can be reapplied several times during the tattooing process as needed.

To Numb or Not to Numb?

As mentioned earlier, there are plenty of tattoo artists, enthusiasts and collectors who believe that it's wrong to deaden the pain of the tattooing process. If you take that attitude as an artist though, you may lose yourself some decent-paying jobs, and the negative word-of-mouth that could ensue may be even more detrimental to your business than losing a few clients with low pain thresholds. It's much better to be flexible and meet each client's individual needs to ensure they have a positive tattooing experience. Doing so will win you more happy customers and more referrals, than being unyielding about minimizing squeamish clients' pain.

If you're a consumer who desperately wants to work with a tattoo artist who doesn't believe in using topical anesthetics, don't fret! You can buy one or two topical anesthetic products through us, use them at home, and bear through the tattooing process much more comfortably without your artist ever knowing.

Tattoo Anesthetic Options

Whether you're a tattoo artist looking for tattoo anesthetic options to numb pain-sensitive clients' skin or an individual who wants to be prepared when you go to get a tattoo, we have tattoo anesthetic and numbing options to meet your needs. Many of our tattoo anesthetic options come in single bottles or jars, as well as display cases, so you can buy a bottle for yourself or a pack to stock your shop. Learn about some of our most popular tattoo anesthetic options below, or visit our Tattoo Anesthetic & Numbing Options section to see every topical anesthetic cream and spray we offer.

Tattoo Anesthetic Creams

We have a variety of tattoo anesthetic creams to numb the skin and keep it moisturized during the tattooing process. Choose from tattoo anesthetic cream options like Tattoo Soothe, Feel Better Now and Instant Numb Cream.

Recovery Numb Tattoo Anesthetic Cream

Recovery Numb Tattoo Anesthetic Cream is a vegan-friendly topical anesthetic that can dramatically reduce your clients' sensitivity to pain during the tattooing process, cosmetic procedures, laser tattoo removal, and more. It contains 5% lidocaine--the highest percentage of topical anesthetic that the FDA allows in over-the-counter numbing creams. This highly-effective formula reduces inflammation and eases pain for up to six hours.

Each tube of Recovery Numb Tattoo Anesthetic Cream contains 2.2 oz. of numbing cream that takes effect within 15 minutes of application. (Cases of 12 2.2 oz. tubes are also available.) For maximum relief, have clients apply a layer at home before coming in to get tattooed, or apply it in your shop 15-20 minutes before you begin the tattooing process. You can enhance the effects of Recovery Numb by wrapping the treated skin with plastic cling wrap for optimal absorption.

Tattoo Soothe Numbing Cream

Tattoo Soothe is a topical anesthetic cream that's available in 15g jars, 8g jars, and cases of 12 8g jars. This topical numbing cream relieves pain, swelling and bleeding during the tattooing process. Tattoo Soothe is a fast-acting formula comprised of 5% lidocaine, tetracaine and epinephrine that allows clients to relax during extended tattooing sessions. When you're working on more sensitive areas, like underarms and ribs, Tattoo Soothe will sufficiently numb the skin so your clients flinch less and end up with better-looking tattoos. Apply Tattoo Soothe to your clients' skin 15-25 minutes before you start tattooing, and re-apply this numbing cream throughout the tattooing process to keep clients comfortable for hours on end.

Note: Tattoo Soothe cream and Tattoo Soothe gel can be used in combination for enhanced relief that lasts throughout the tattooing process.

Feel Better Now Topical Anesthetic Cream

Feel Better Now is a high-quality topical tattoo anesthetic cream that comes in a 15g jar. It contains 5% lidocaine, 20% benzocaine, and 4% tetracaine for optimal numbing. Apply Feel Better Now topical anesthetic cream to clients' skin 15-25 minutes before you start tattooing to minimize their discomfort. It can really help ease the sting of starting the tattooing process.

Use Feel Better Now topical anesthetic cream in combination with Feel Better Now numbing gel to amplify the effects of the anesthetic and provide clients with an additional layer of comfort while you tattoo them. You only need to wait 3-5 minutes after applying a secondary layer of Feel Better Now gel over top of the initial application of Feel Better Now numbing cream before resuming tattooing.

Instant Numb Cream

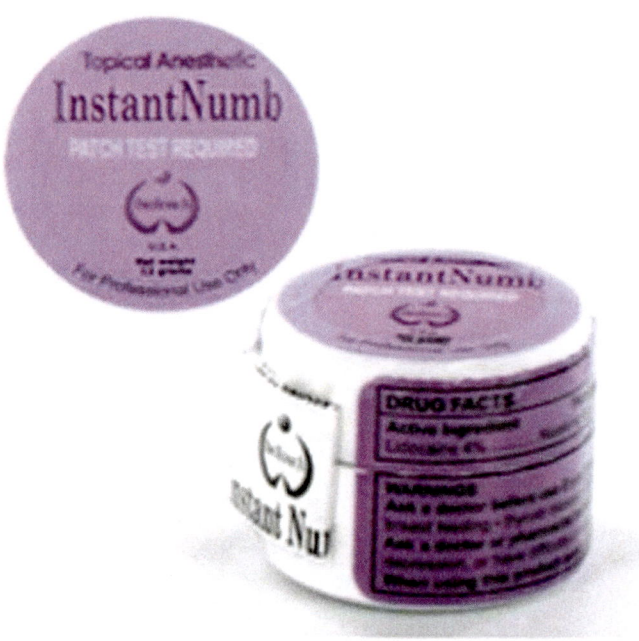

Instant Numb Cream is a strong tattoo anesthetic designed specifically for relieving discomfort in sensitive areas like the lips, eyes and eyebrows during permanent makeup procedures. Instant Numb cosmetic tattoo anesthetic cream contains tea tree oil, aloe and 4% lidocaine, making it a superior numbing agent that also refreshes, cools and soothes the skin. It comes in a 12g jar for multiple applications. You can combine InstantNumbCream with BioGel to control swelling and bleeding during the procedure.

Bactine Antiseptic & Anesthetic Spray

Bactine is a tried and true graddaddy of tattoo anesthetic spray options that doubles as an antiseptic. It contains 2.5% lidocaine and 0.13% benzalkonium chloride, as well as purified water, fragrances and other inactive ingredients. Bactine anesthetic spray relieves pain on contact with no sting. You can use it to minimize the discomfort of tattooing and prevent infection from minor cuts, scrapes and burns. Bactine soothes the skin, promotes healing, reduces redness, and minimizes swelling caused by tattoo procedures. You can spray it on, apply it with gauze or use it to enhance your tattoo skin prep solutions. Bactine comes in 5 oz. bottles and is intended for external use only.

Derma Numb Tattoo Anesthetic Spray

Derma Numb tattoo anesthetic spray is a proven formula that enables clients to more thoroughly enjoy the tattooing experience. It contains yarrow root and yucca glauca root--two ingredients known for their healing, numbing, cell rejuvenation, sterilizing, and anti-inflammatory properties. Derma Numb also contains lidocaine to boost its numbing abilities; the lidocaine makes Derma Numb start working within 90 seconds of application.

Derma Numb was designed specifically as a tattoo anesthetic spray, so you won't have to worry about it negatively impacting ink colors or the healing process. You can purchase Derma Numb tattoo anesthetic spray in 1 oz. bottles or cases of 12 1 oz. bottles. Reapply it as often as necessary to keep your clients comfortable while you tattoo them.

System One Tattoo Ice Numbing Spray

System One's Tattoo Ice topical tattoo anesthetic spray was developed specifically for use during the tattooing process. It's a fast-acting formula that reduces redness, irritation and discomfort. Tattoo Ice numbing spray starts working just 90 seconds after application, and it can be reapplied as often as necessary throughout the tattooing process. It contains 3.5% lidocaine and is safe on all skin types. Pick up an 8 oz. bottle of System One Tattoo Ice Topical Anesthetic Numbing Spray to make long tattooing sessions more comfortable for your clients.

CORINNE ASCH

Tattoo Anesthetic Gels

When you need to boost the effects of a tattoo anesthetic cream, you can typically add a layer of an anesthetic gel over top to further numb clients' skin and make the tattooing experience more enjoyable for them. Most tattoo anesthetic gels make great topical numbing agents on their own, too. We offer a wide variety of tattoo anesthetic gel options to give you the choices you crave, including numbing gels by Derma Numb, Tattoo Soothe, Hush, and Feel Better Now.

Derma Numb Tattoo Anesthetic Gel

Derma Numb tattoo anesthetic gel is available in 2 oz. bottles and cases of 12 2 oz. bottles. Each bottle contains 4% lidocaine, menthol, yarrow extract, yucca glauca root extract, aloe, and other ingredients to thoroughly numb and soothe your clients' skin during the tattooing process. Derma Numb anesthetic gel is easy to apply, and it's formulated with natural ingredients that are safe for all skin types and that won't impact ink colors or shading. As an added benefit, Derma Numb tattoo anesthetic gel also acts as an anti-inflammatory and skin cell rejuvenator that opens skin cells and yields better tattoo results.

Apply a generous amount of Derma Numb anesthetic gel one hour before you start tattooing. For best results, wrap the treated skin with plastic cling wrap to seal in the product and ensure optimal absorption. When the numbing effects start to wear off, spray the skin with Derma Numb tattoo anesthetic spray to ensure your client's comfort for the duration of the procedure.

Tattoo Soothe Topical Anesthetic Gel

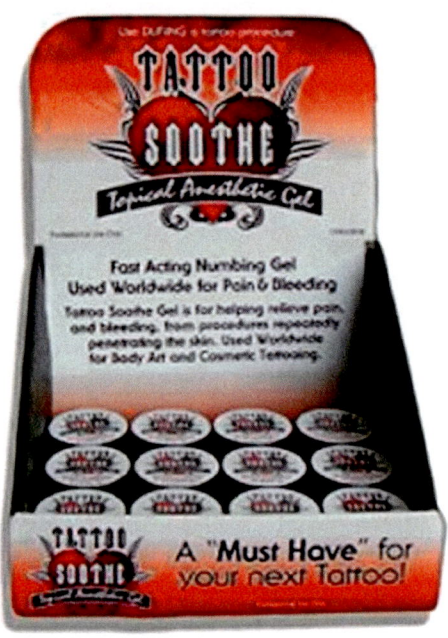

Tattoo Soothe topical anesthetic gel comes in 1 oz. bottles, 10g jars, and cases of 12 10g jars. This topical numbing gel relieves pain, minimizes swelling, and reduces bleeding from tattoo procedures. It has a fast-acting formula consisting of 5% lidocaine, tetracaine and epinephrine that allows clients to relax and enjoy the tattooing process with less discomfort.

Tattoo Soothe topical anesthetic gel is intended for use in combination with Tattoo Soothe topical numbing cream. Apply a thin layer of the cream over the area you'll be tattooing 15-25 minutes before you begin. If your client is still uncomfortable after you've made a few passes with your tattoo machine, add a thin layer of Tattoo Soothe Gel over the area, wait 3-5 minutes, and resume tattooing. You can reapply the numbing gel one or two more times during the tattooing process, as needed for your client's optimal comfort.

Hush Topical Numbing Gel

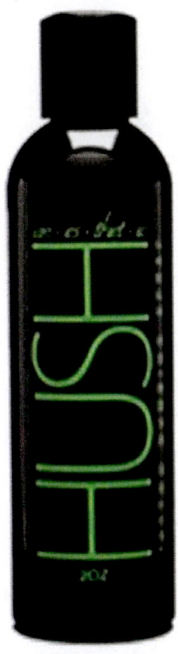

Like Hush topical anesthetic cream, Hush topical numbing gel comes in 2 oz. bottles, 4 oz. bottles, cases of 12 2 oz. bottles, and cases of 12 4 oz. bottles. This special formula is intended for use before tattooing as well as prior to laser tattoo removal and piercings. It's a clear, non-oily gel consisting of a blend of botanical extracts that numb the skin, like menthol and comfrey root extract, 4% lidocaine, aloe to soothe the skin, and other calming, nourishing ingredients. Hush tattoo anesthetic gel is safe for all skin types. It won't affect ink colors, it reduces redness, and it minimizes inflammation during the tattooing process.

Apply a thick layer of Hush tattoo anesthetic gel to the skin before you begin tattooing. Spread it evenly over the area, and reapply more gel along the edges. Wrap the area with plastic cling wrap and let it sit for an hour for maximum absorption. You can then remove the plastic wrap, prep the skin as you would normally, and start tattooing.

Feel Better Now Topical Anesthetic Gel

Feel Better Now numbing gel is a great tool for cosmetic tattoo artists. It's formulated specifically for use on sensitive facial areas where permanent makeup is applied, like eyebrows and lips, and it's safe to use around the eyes. This numbing gel contains 5% lidocaine, tetracaine and epinephrine to relieve pain, minimize swelling, and reduce bleeding from cosmetic tattoo procedures. It can also be used for laser hair removal and other cosmetic procedures that can be harsh on the skin.

Feel Better Now numbing gel is intended for use in combination with Feel Better Now topical anesthetic cream. Apply the cream to a client's skin 15-25 minutes before you begin a cosmetic tattoo procedure. Then, after you've made a few initial passes, ask your client about their pain level. If they're finding the procedure uncomfortable, add a thin layer of Feel Better Now numbing gel over the area, wait 3-5 minutes, and resume tattooing. Add additional layers of Feel Better Now topical anesthetic gel as needed to give your clients optimal comfort during permanent makeup procedures.

Tattoo Anesthetic Soaps

In addition to tattoo anesthetic sprays, creams and gels, you can now get pain-relieving foam soap from H2Ocean! H2Ocean's Nothing pain-relieving soap is specially formulated to clean the skin and relieve pain during tattoo procedures. It prevents swelling, distortion, and ink color alteration. Simply wash your clients' skin with this antibacterial anesthetic foam soap to clean, disinfect and soothe it before you start tattooing.

H2Ocean's Nothing pain-relieving soap consists of 5% lidocaine, 0.13% benzalkonium chloride, purified water, aloe juice, sea salt, and other inactive ingredients that clean, soothe and nourish the skin. This soap will make the tattooing process more comfortable for your clients, and they can take a bottle home with them to minimize discomfort and clean tattoos thoroughly during the healing process. H2Ocean's Nothing pain-relieving soap is available in 1.7 oz. bot-tles and cases of 24 1.7 oz. bottles.

A word about H2Ocean anesthetic soap

It is enriched with aloe vera and is an all-natural anti-microbial soap that is not harsh like other anti-bacterial soaps and it effectively stops the onset of excessive drying and scabbing. Perfect to use throughout the healing process.

CHAPTER 8
MEASURING THE BROWS

Measuring the brows is another area where there are a lot of opposing opinions. Admittedly, there are many ways of properly measuring the brows and everyone has their favorite technique. You will naturally find yours.

At first it seems complicated and confusing, but its one of those things that after you've done it a few times it makes sense and becomes easy to do. You will eventually forget why this ever seemed complicated.

Some seasoned microbladers prefer to do it free-hand; and although there is nothing wrong with that, as a beginner, it may be more prudent to let the measures be your guide. It takes most of the guess work out of brow designing and will prevent big variations between the brows. The measuring of the brows is to the microblader what a safety net is to the trapeze artist.

So, let's demystify brow measuring and take a look at how easy it is to get a symmetrical look.

1. Make a line in between the brows, using the center of nose as your guide.

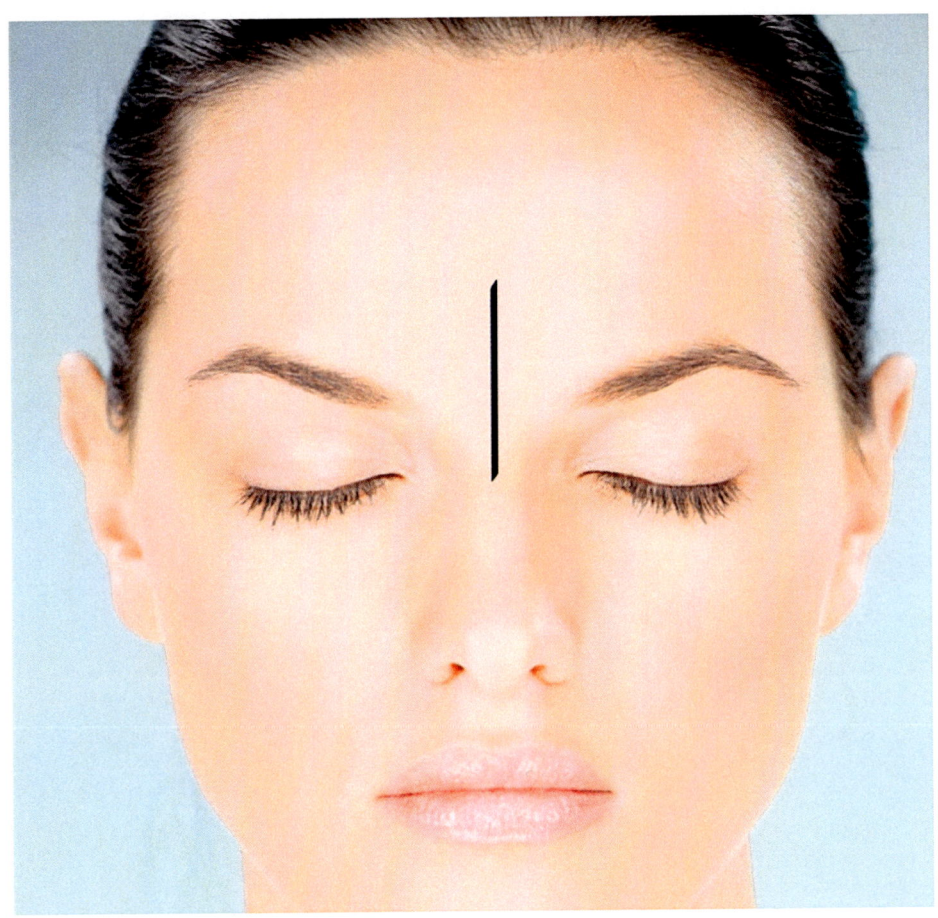

2. Here you get to choose where you would like the brow to start. For a wider brow, you can start at the middle. Your choice should depend on 2 factors: 1. The client's eye distance, i.e., if her eyes are wide set, then the closer brow may be best and if her eyes are close set then the wider brow may be what is needed. 2. The desired look, i.e., a thicker, stronger brow. Make a mark.

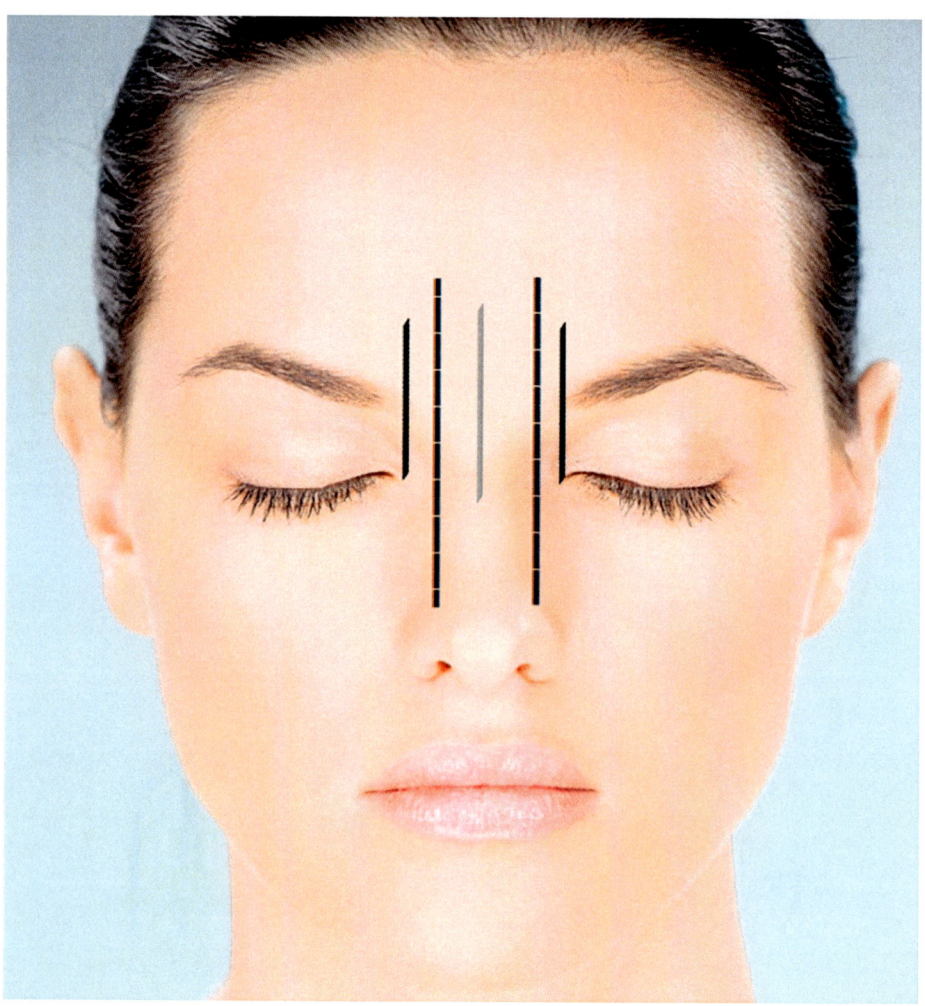

3. Next, we are going to define where the brow ends. You will make an imaginary straight line from the outer nose to the outside of the eye to the outer brow. Any straight object will work as a ruler. Make a mark.

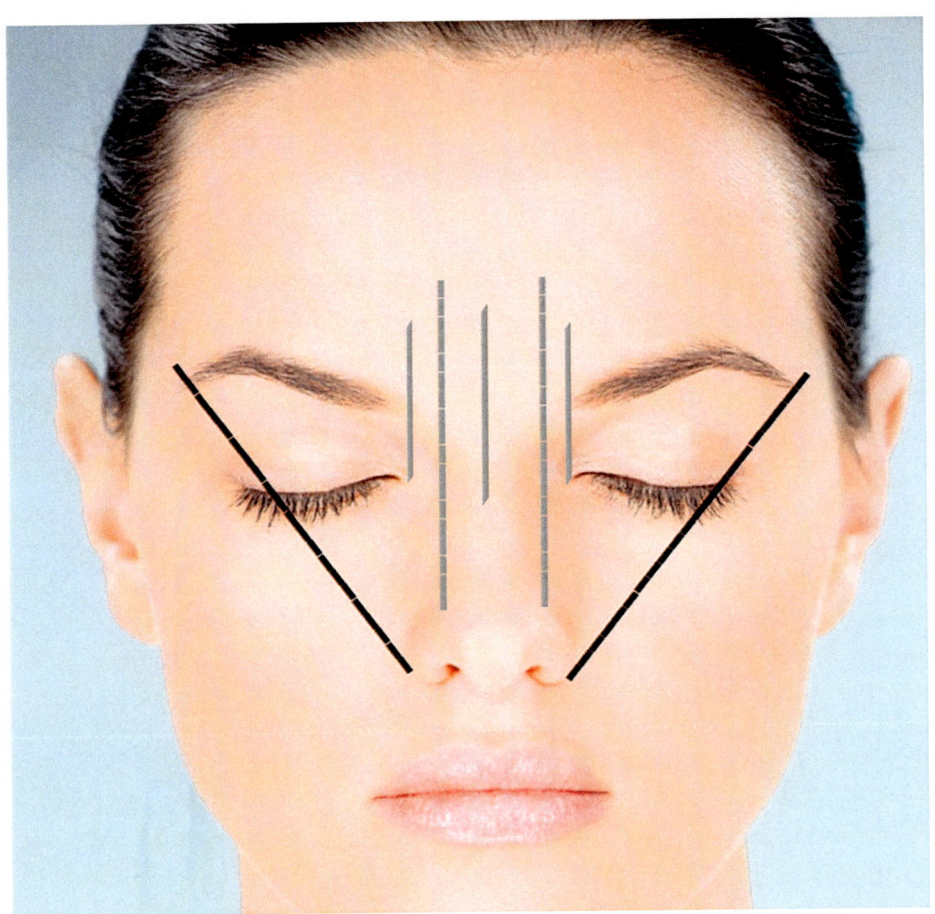

4. To find the height of where your arch should be and to make sure the arch will be at the same height on both sides, feel where the highest point of the brow bone is and make a straight line from one brow to the other. At this point, I like to switch to string and kohl to make drawing the lines a breeze.

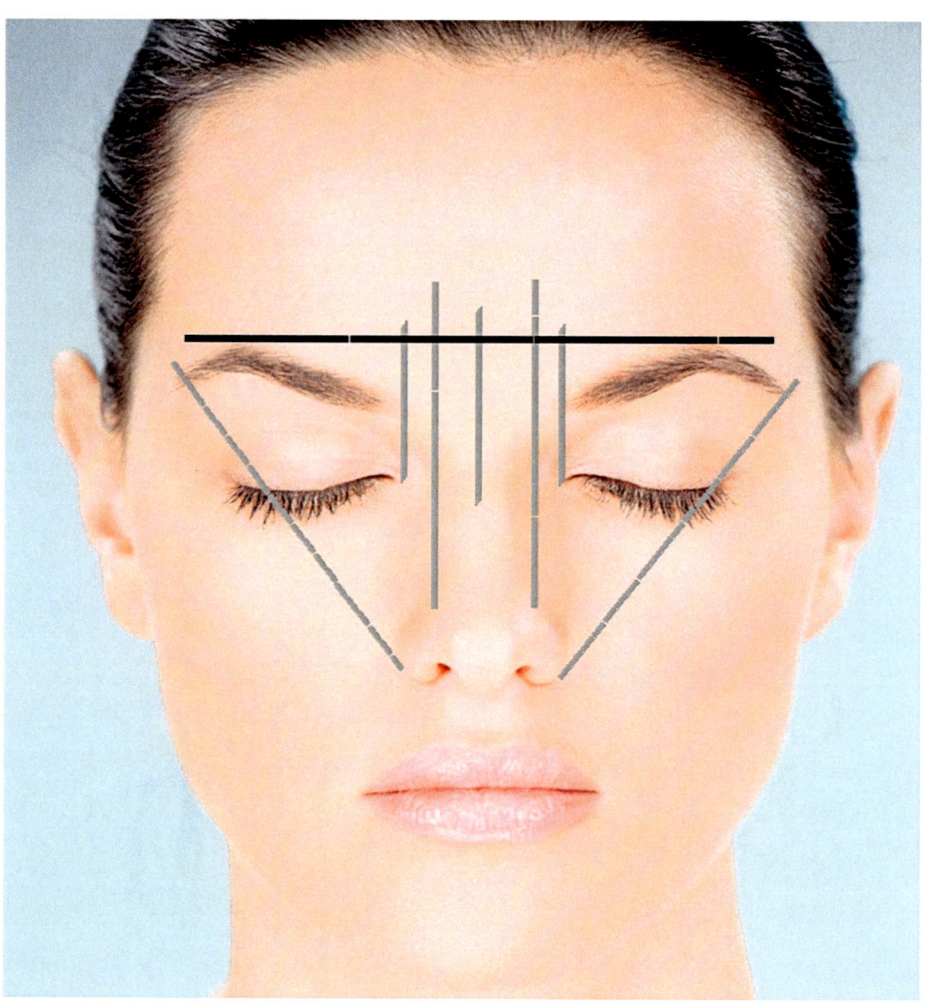

5. Now that we have a beginning, an end, and the height, let's find where the arch should be. There are many ways to do this. A caliper is a big help at this stage. Here, I will give you 3 ways to achieve your goal. One way to do this is to measure the brow from the first mark to the end mark. The 2/3 mark is where your arch will be. Another way to find the arch is to measure the distance between the tear ducts and use that measurement to determine where your arch will be. Make a mark.

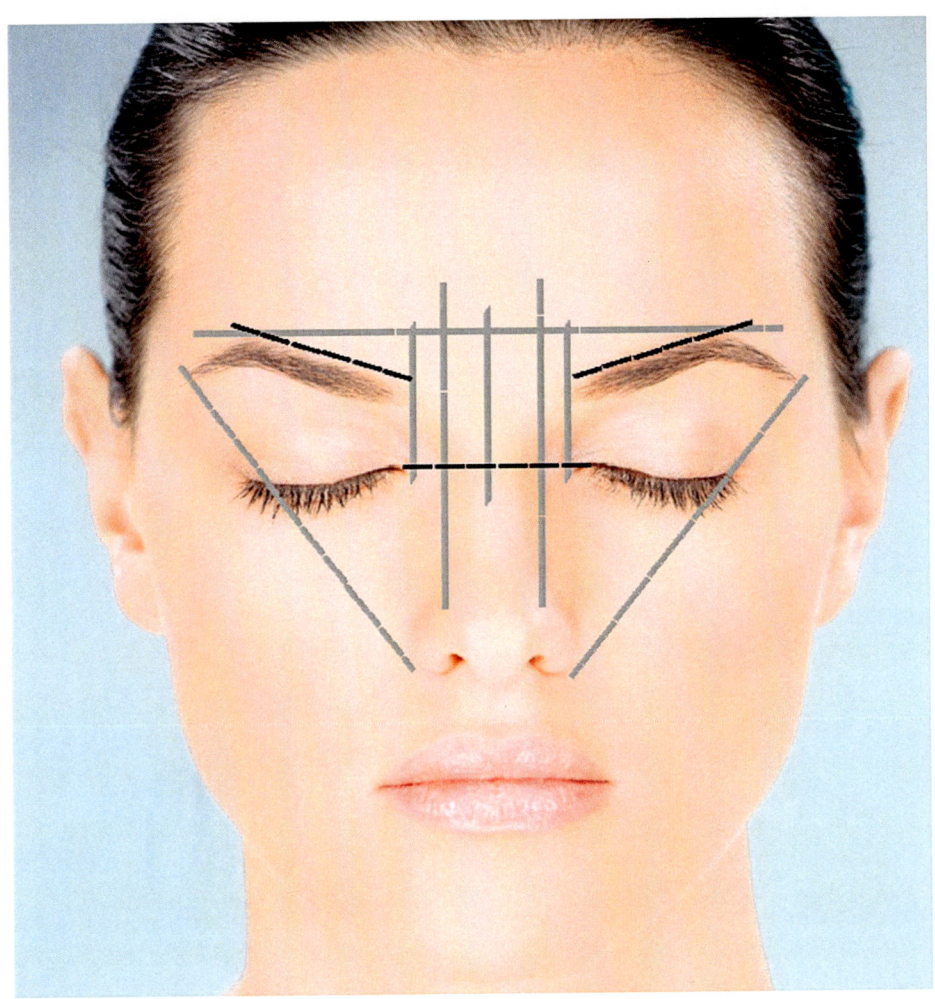

A third way is to make an imaginary straight line from the outer nostril through the iris of the eye to the brow. Make a mark.

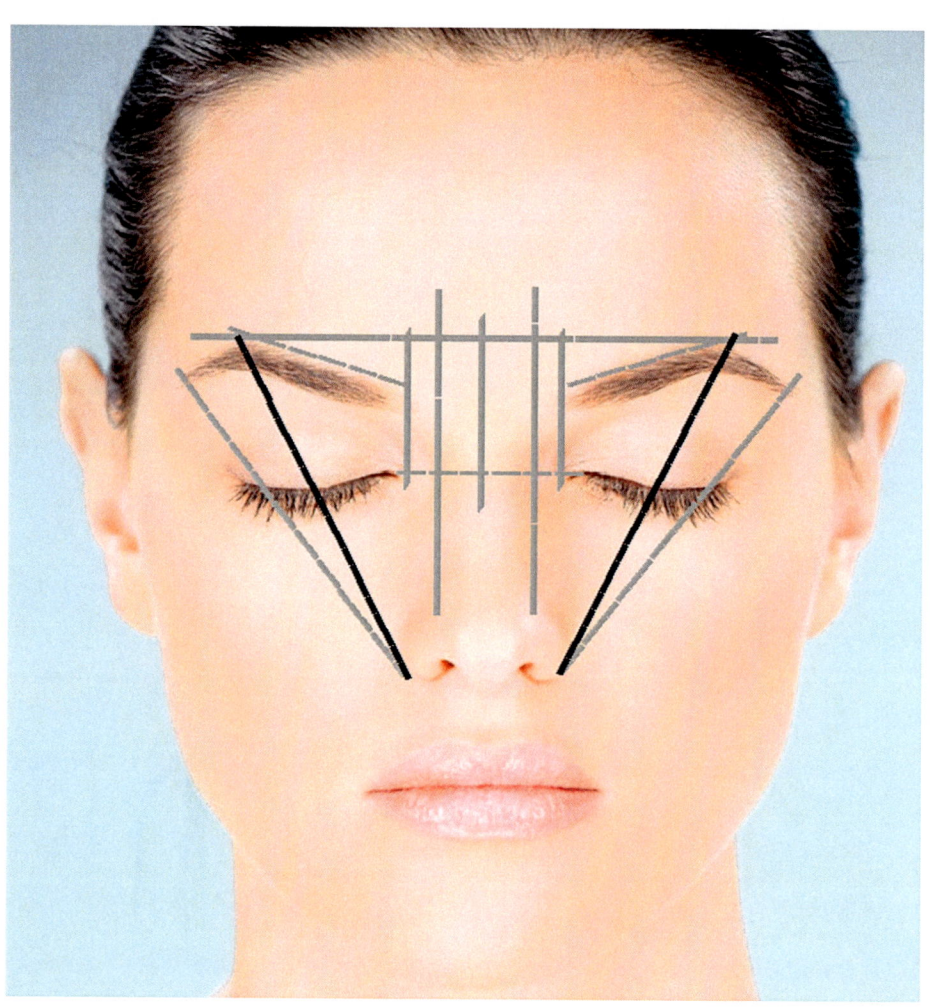

6. Feel the front brow bone and feel for the lowest part. Now make a straight line accross the bottom of both brows. The end of the brow may be higher than the beginning of brow, but never lower.

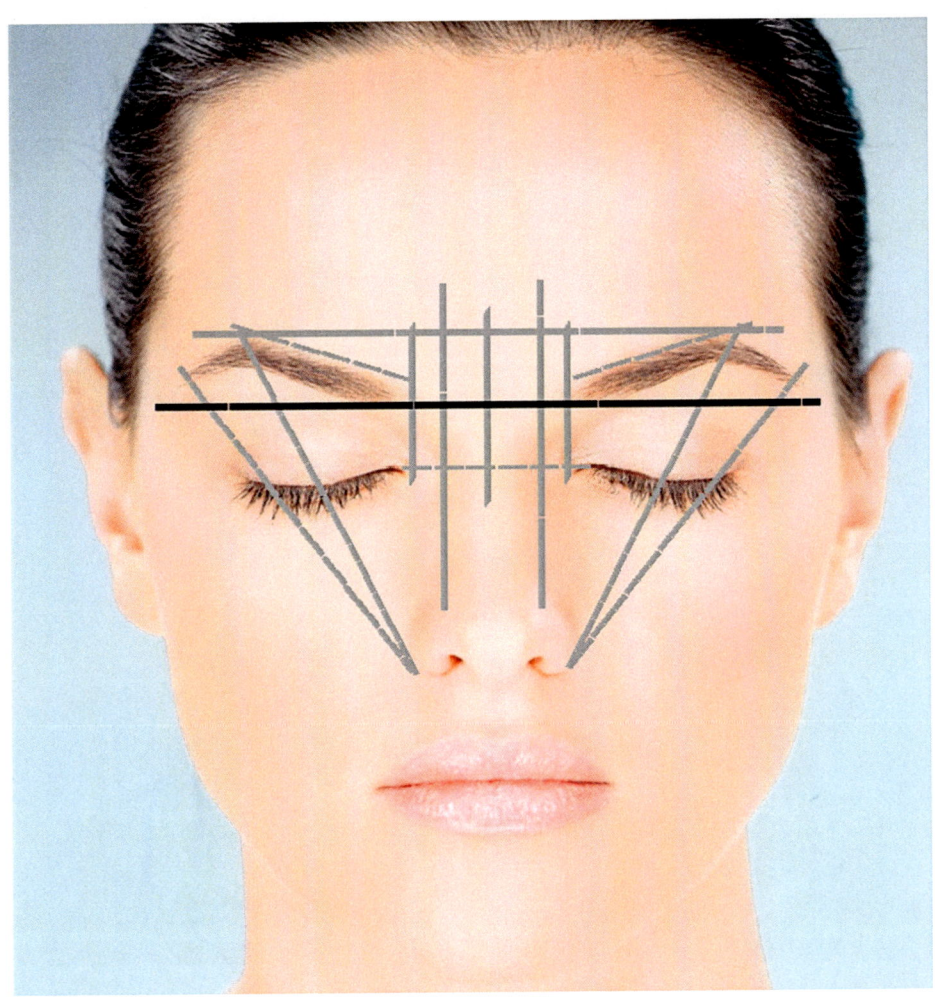

7. This is where you decide on the thickness of the brow. Draw a line on the upper (bulb) of the brow at the desired thickness.

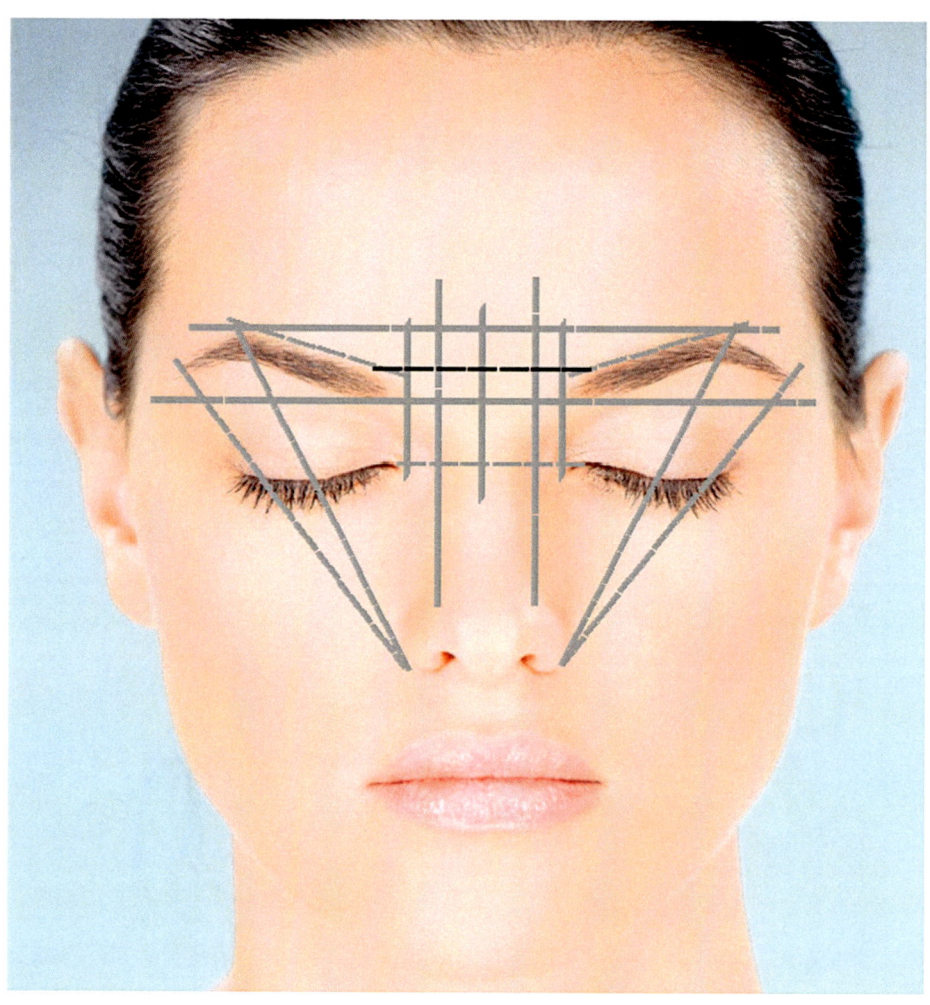

8. With your string or ruler, draw a straight line from the bottom of one bulb to opposing arch. Repeat on the other side.

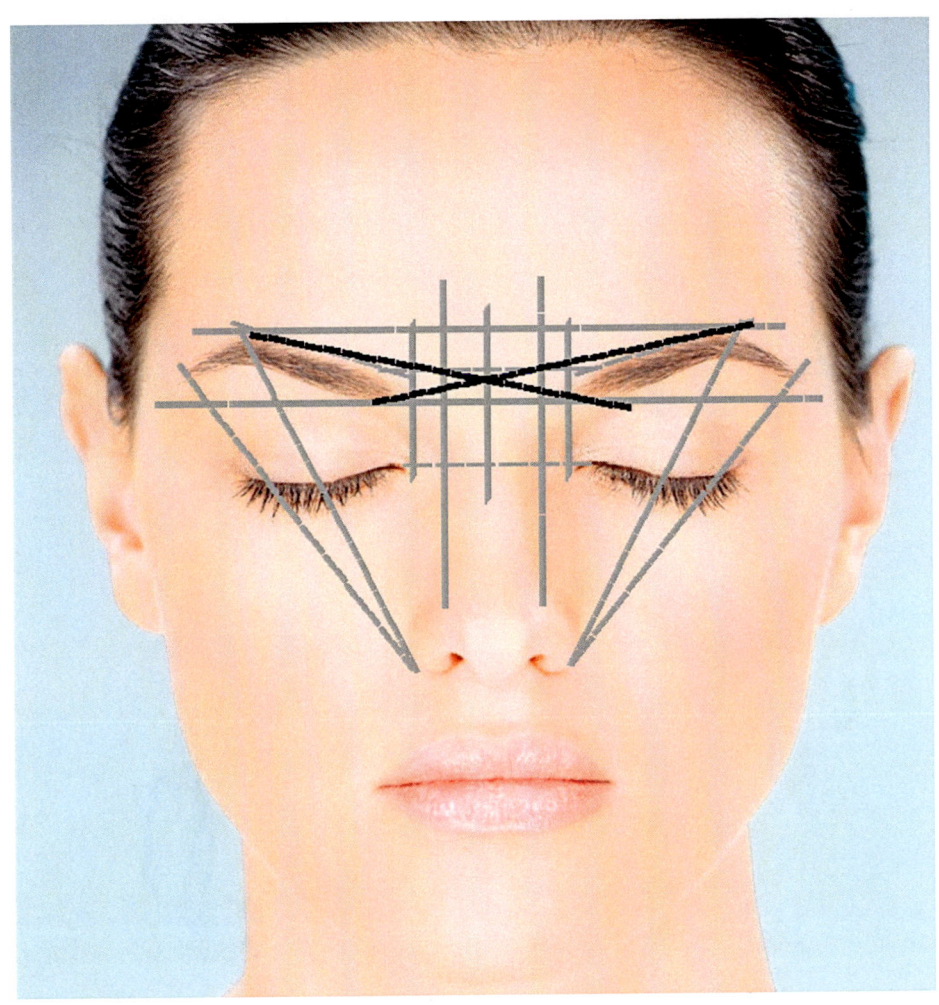

9. Draw a line from top of the arch to end of brow. Repeat on the other side.

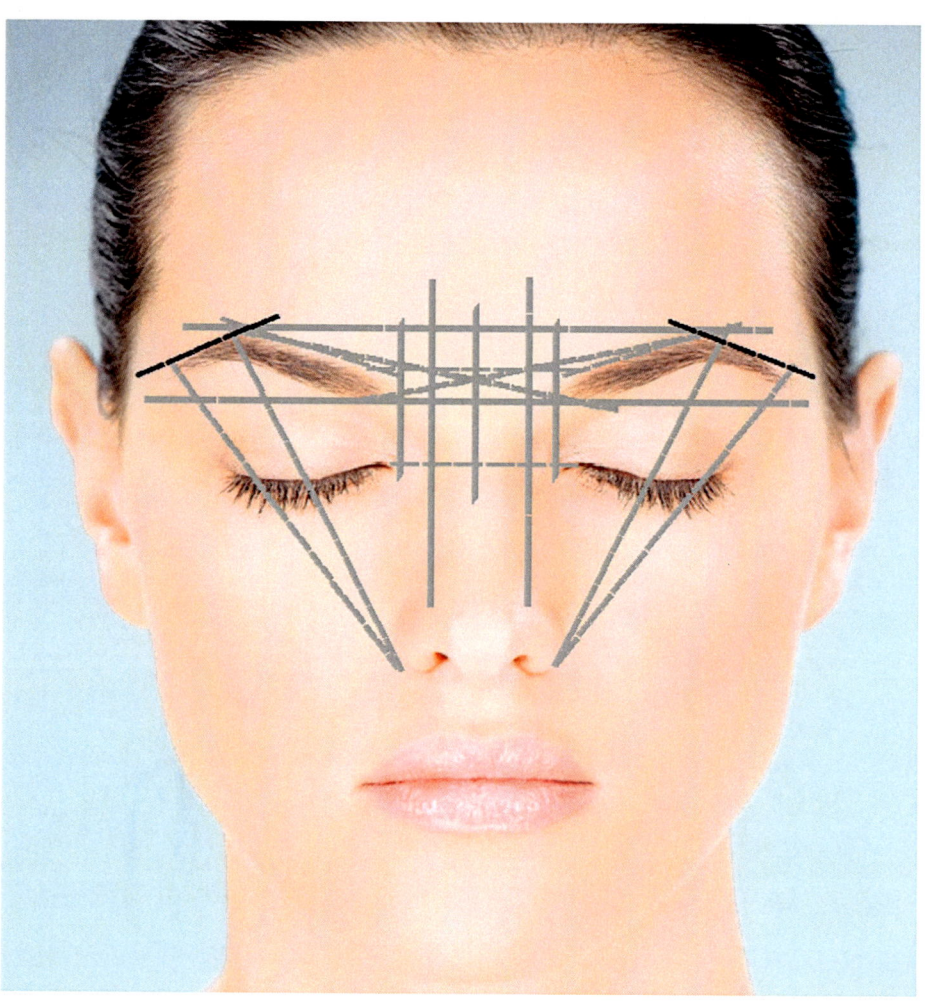

THE MICROBLADING BIBLE

10. Draw a line from the bottom of brow bulb to the arch. Repeat on other side.

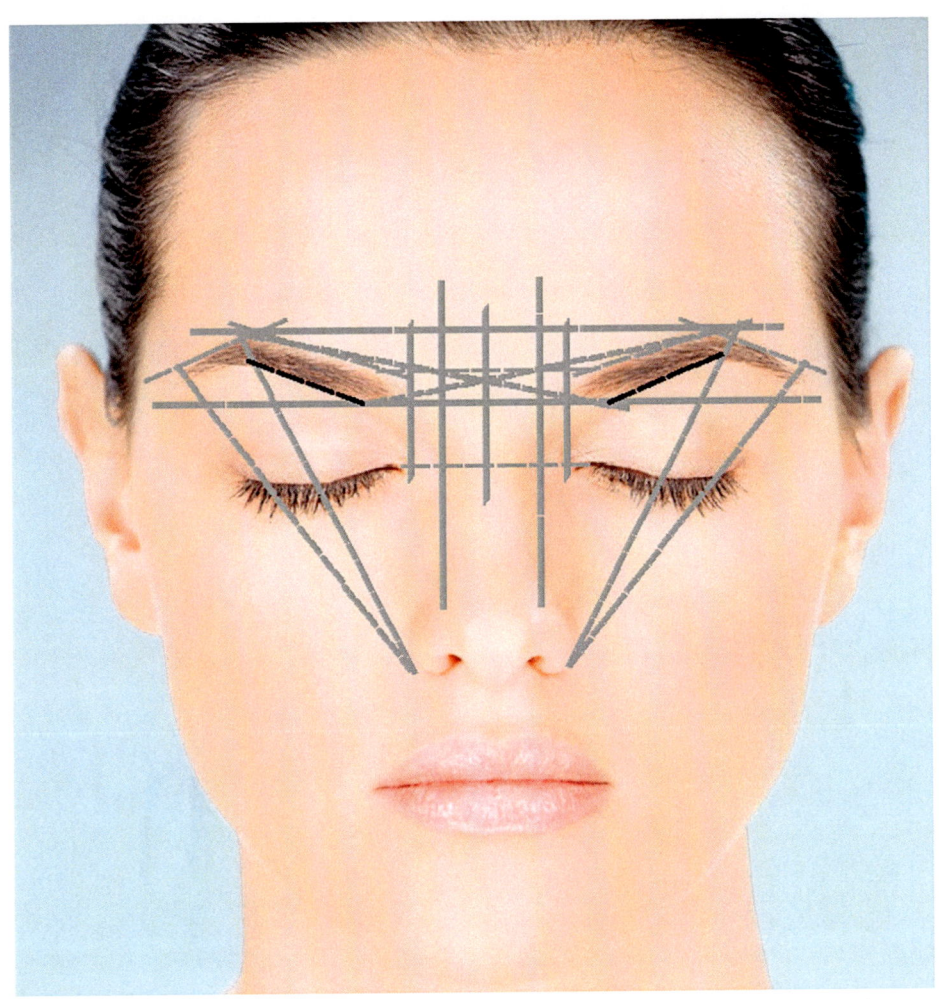

11. Draw a line from the last line drawn to the end of the brow. Repeat on the other side.

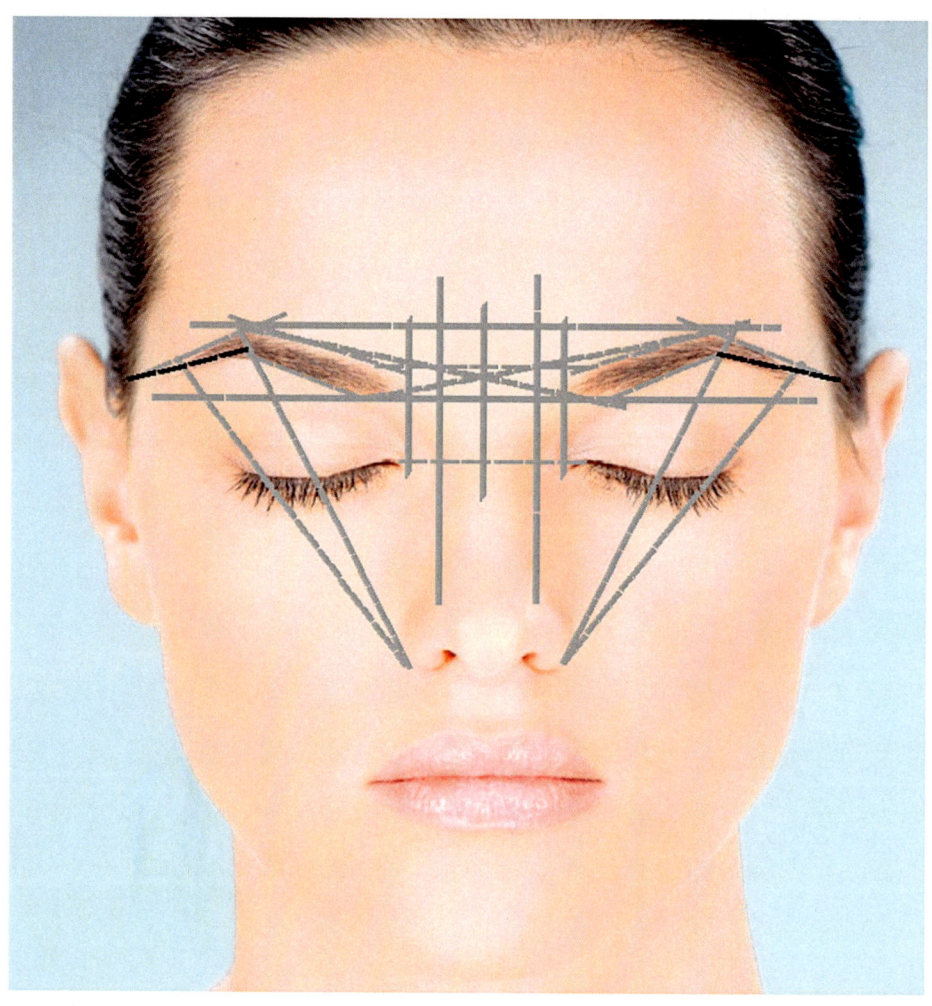

At this point, drawing in the brows should be easy, especially if you've been practicing drawing brows freehand.

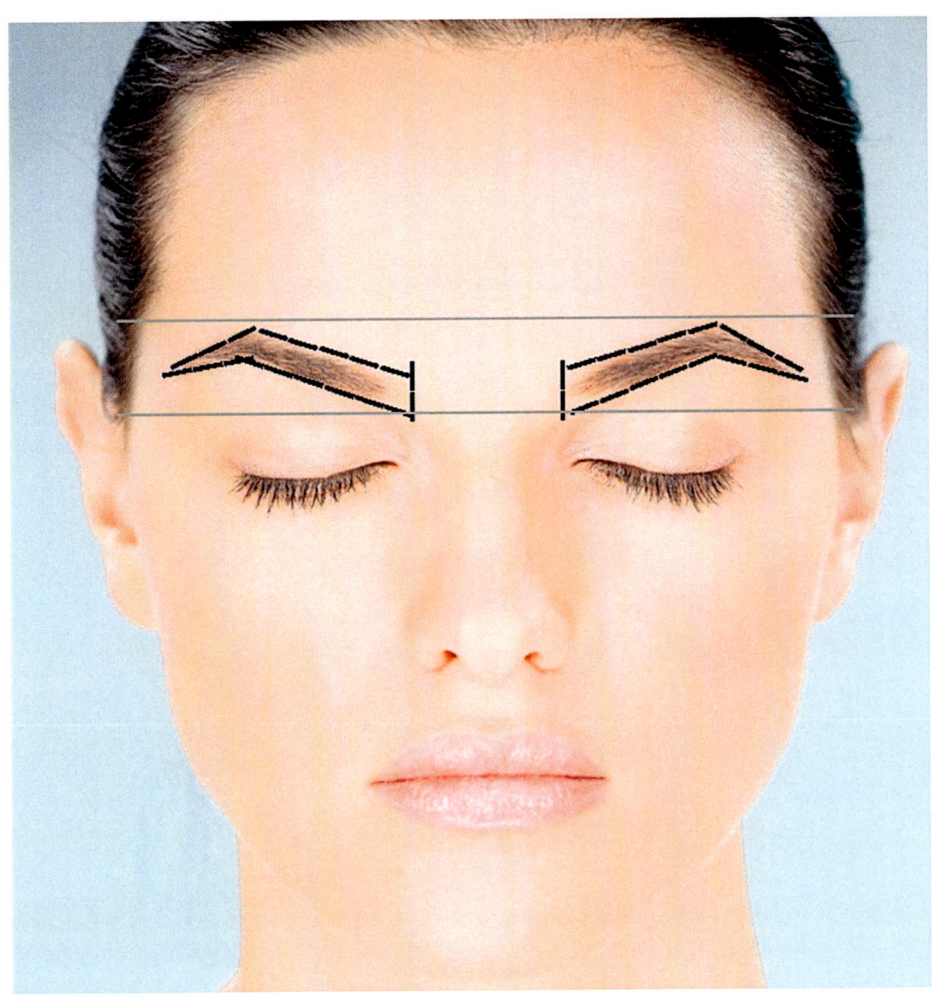

Anatomy of a brow

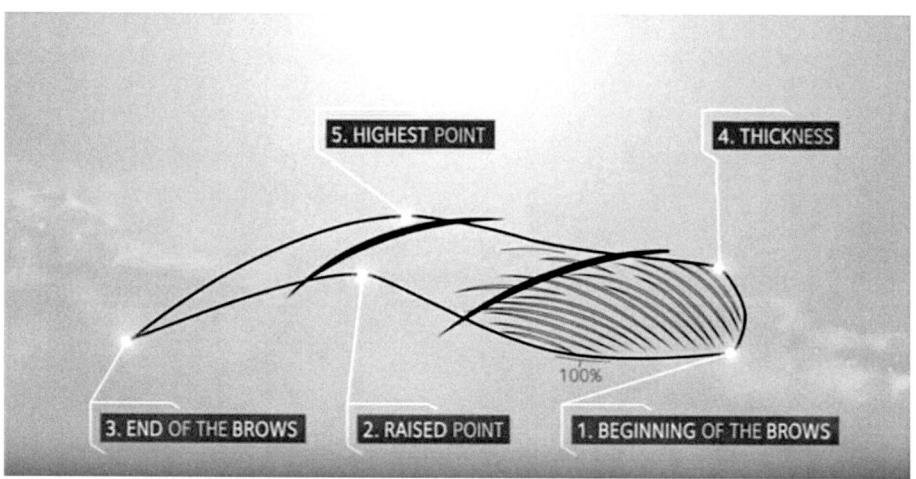

1. As a general rule, the beginning of the brows should be the first ¼ of the brow.

2. Raised point of the underneath of brow should come at the 2/3 mark of the brow.

3. End of brow is the thinnest part of brow and should never be lower than the bulb.

4. The bulb is the thickest part of the brow.

5. Highest point of the brow should come at 2/3 mark of the brow.

Phibrow has a wonderfully helpful measuring app that is free of charge. You can see how it works on Youtube.

CHAPTER 9
CHOOSING THE RIGHT BLADE FOR THE JOB

I wasn't taught much about blades in my training. I was told use this one first and then this one second. I didn't know you could use different blades for different effects and that different skin types require different blades.

Some technicians will use the same blade throughout the procedure and some will change the type of blade they use on the second and third pass. What we call blades in microblading are actually needles placed closely together to create a kind of blade.

Do you know your blades and what they do?

Well, read on and I'll explain the different blades available to us and what they can do for you.

Blades come in flexi and hard blades and go from 7 pins all the way to 28, going from thin to thicker as the numbers go up. In general, you would do your first passes with a thinner blade and do your ensuing passes with thicker blades to deposit more pigment. Again, these are general rules. Let your creativity be your guide.

Below are the most commonly used needles/blades. Perfect for the beginners and advanced practitioners.

7-pin blade – the single row 7-pin blade will be your finest of all the blades. This blade will be good for creating shorter, thinner hairs. It is a good blade for thin brows and for little in-between hairs. Good for detailed work.

12-pin blade – Used to create medium length eyebrow hairs of medium thickness. This is the blade most often used.

14-pin blade – Used to create long eyebrow hairs of medium to above medium thickness. This blade is good to create thicker brows.

U Shape blade – 18 super fine single needles- good for drawing curvy hairs and recommended for the more experienced technician.

There are blades with one row of needles and blades with double rows of needles. The single row blades will be flexible and create finer strokes. The double row blades create stronger strokes and are good for the thicker and oilier skin. Harder blades are good for oily skin or for skin in the Fitzpatrick range of between 3–6. Hard blades are good for bolder results. Hard blades will go deeper with less pressure. Good for thick or oily skins. Thinner, more flexible blades are recommended for skin in the Fitzpatrick range of 1-3. Older skin is almost always thinner and offers less resistance so a finer more flexible needle is best.

The less needles present, the thinner the strokes will be and, the more needles there are, the thicker the strokes will be. Also, the smaller the needle configuration used for the eyebrow procedure, the more ash (and ash is always cooler and darker) the healed procedure will appear. Why? Because the smaller needles slice through the skin more effectively and generally place pigment deeper. The use of larger needle configurations has less of a slicing effect and for lack of a better word, more or less plummet pigment into the skin, thus placing the pigment slightly closer too light and further from direct relationship with the bloodstream (blue). Pigment that remains closer to the surface of the skin will reflect more light and appear less cool than pigment that resides deeper in the skin.

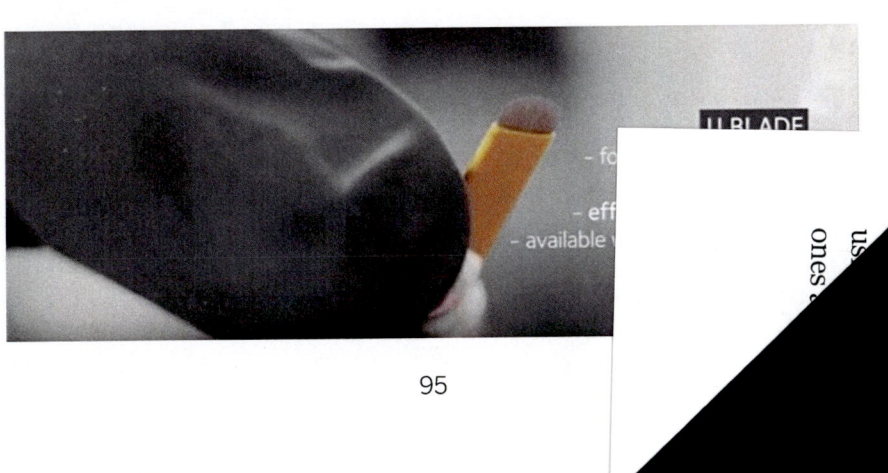

Following is an article by Deluxe Brows on choosing the right blades and checking your work.

ARTICLE

How to choose the right microblades / microblading needles – Deluxe Brows®

TIP No. 1 HOW TO CHOOSE GOOD QUALITY MICROBLADING NEEDLES / BLADES

Almost for every new microblading artist and sometimes even for those with experience, it is really difficult to analyze and understand which kind of microblading needles/blades we need to use for our treatments. I did the research regarding this long time ago and during our training, I explained all the differences between the several kinds of needles. However, I decided to share with all of you the most important tips that my company and I mostly use while choosing the needles. I hope this will help you to make your own decisions.

Microblading treatments and trainings are taking the industry by storm. Each and every company trying to stay on top, offering the new tools, needles, pigments and all kinds of new items that helps this industry to grow.

With this post, I will share one of the most important tips, which will help you to choose your microblades/ microblading needles.

I will be talking only about the flexible needle this time, which I am using mostly, but please take a note the same tip, can be used for hard as well. It does not matter which shape you prefer oval or angled.

The visual test can be very insignificant. As you can see in the picture on the right, the blades and needles inside look almost similar, but in reality they are completely different. So how do we know which of them are good or bad?

Have you ever experienced that your strokes are not as clear, and pigment on the stroke spreads unevenly? Well, this is very common when you have luck of experience or wrong knowledge regarding right pressure. However, all these things can also happen if you are using poor quality blades. When the needles in the blade are not fixed in the correct way, it is very easy to bend them and have two strokes instead of one (Blade No.1). If the skin is so thin, sometimes you cannot even realize that needles are bending, you only will see the unclear stroke when it's done. When your strokes heal the lines won't be crispy. With these types of blades, it is more difficult to repeat the strokes.

What should you do to make sure? How to avoid double lines and get crispy results? The first and best solution is to use good quality nickel needles that are well fixed in with each other.

You can do a quick test on the artificial skin. Place the needle in your manual tool and try to draw the stroke gently. The needles in blade cannot move or bend while you are sliding (like the Blade No.1)

You can also check your blade by pressing it on the side with your nail. The needles cannot move as well.

The needles in good quality blade will be stable (like the Blade No.2) despite the fact that blade itself is flexible. It will be easier to draw and the result will be always the same – clear and crispy strokes!

TIP No.2 HOW TO CHOOSE THE RIGHT THICKNESS OF THE BLADE

The other important thing is to understand what is the best thickness of your blades and how it affects the results.

The other important thing is to understand what is the best thickness of your blades and how it affects the results.

The main important thing is that thinner blades are more sharp then thicker blades. To understand why they are sharper, have a look on the left picture were you could see Blade Nr.1, which has thicker needles, and Blade Nr.2, which has thinner needles. As thinner the needles are in the blade as closer they are together. As closer they are as more sharp the blade is.

If you want to avoid missing parts in your strokes or not to get the results with small dots instead of crispy lines, always choose the right needle for different type of skin.

I do not recommend using 0.3 needles.

TIP NO 3 FILLING AND CHECKING YOUR STROKES

While trying to get your strokes darker with several passes, try to use the blade with fewer needles. You will be able to implant pigment in each part of the stroke easier and more precisely. The new blades for filling in the strokes are 7 pins and are very comfortable to use. Take pictures during the work and use a negative filter to check your work, you will clearly see which parts need more pigment.

Prepared and published by Aleksandra Maniušė – Deluxe Brows®

Here is another article on choosing the right blade/needles, this one written by LovBeauty.

ARTICLE

How to choose a right needle for your microblading treatment?

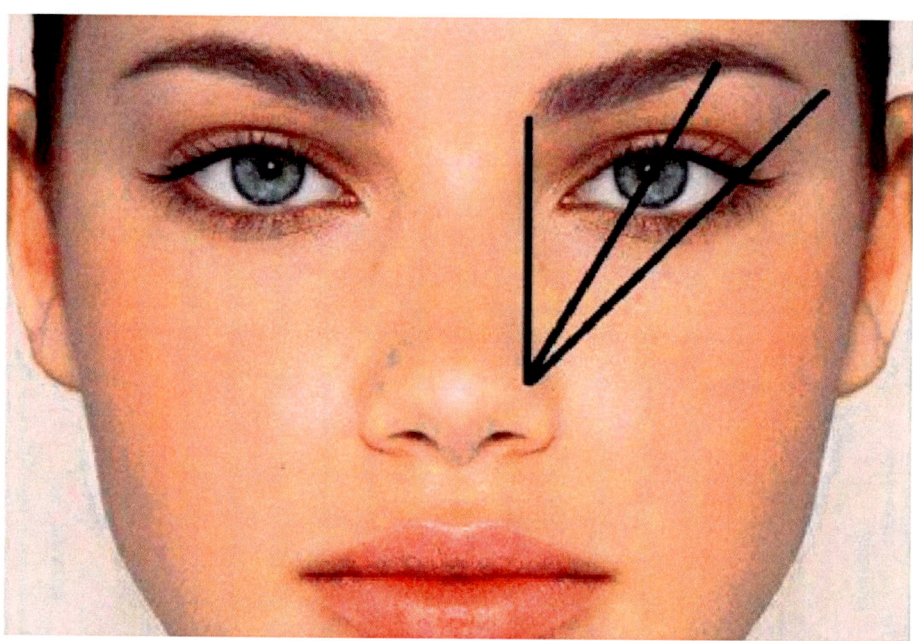

1. The age of the skin: The older the client, the more tissue laxity, collagen and elastin loss you'll notice. Microneedling this aging skin provides a healthier canvas for microblading and this means your hair strokes will stay crisp upon healing.

2. Previous procedures and corrections: You can microblade over old colors and even do corrections. You'll want a bit bigger needle for these cases.

Soft silky needle for 3D eyebrow embroidery

3. Width of hairstroke desired.

4. Pigment you are using.

5. Color carrying capacity of the needle: texture and taper of needles, number of needles and curve of needles are important. More needles, more resistance and you press harder. Higher likelihood of slicing the skin.

6. Skin Resistance: Older skin is less resistant, so use finer needles.

7. The Procedure: Single, curved needles for brow hair strokes. Large, multiple needles for areola, corrections and eyeshadow.

8. Practice makes perfect: You'll develop your very own unique technique over time. Sometimes, you'll switch needles during your case. As you practice, you'll find which needles are the easiest to control and which ones put in the most color. You must know your canvas: the skin, very well.

microblading eyebrows

CHAPTER 10
THE MICROBLADING PROCEDURE

This is the moment you've been waiting for. What your training has been leading up to.

Scared?

Sure, you are. We all were.

It's a scary prospect to cut someone's skin. But have no fear, they are very superficial cuts and there is very little in microblading that can't be fixed. Do your homework and practice, practice, practice. Practice on pads, practice drawing brows, practice using your blade and then practice on friends and family.

Go on the microblading boards and read about other's experiences, it's the next best thing to assisting there is. You can ask all the questions you want there, and these wonderful women will give you all the answers you are looking for.

Sometimes your question will become a debate and that's sooo interesting. They are a passionate and colorful group of girls (and a few guys) from all over the world. There's no getting bored there. It's where I learned the most. So join the microblading facebook groups, find the ones you like best and visit them often. You are guaranteed to learn tons, whether you're a beginner or seasoned professional.

Microblading consists of implanting pigment by creating fine scratches at the upper level of the epidermis, imitating real hair strokes to create a 3D or 6D and powdering effect.

You've taken your before and after pictures. You've drawn on your brows and you and your client agree on the shape and the color. If you're going to numb before the first round of strokes, you've done it and are ready to start.

Every seasoned technician will tell you that getting a crisp, precise stroke is all about the stretching of the skin. A 3-point stretch, to be exact. Two points are with the thumb and pointer of the hand without the blade and the third point is with the pinky of the hand holding the blade. The key is to flatten the skin in 3 opposing directions. The flatter the skin is stretched, the cleaner your strokes will be.

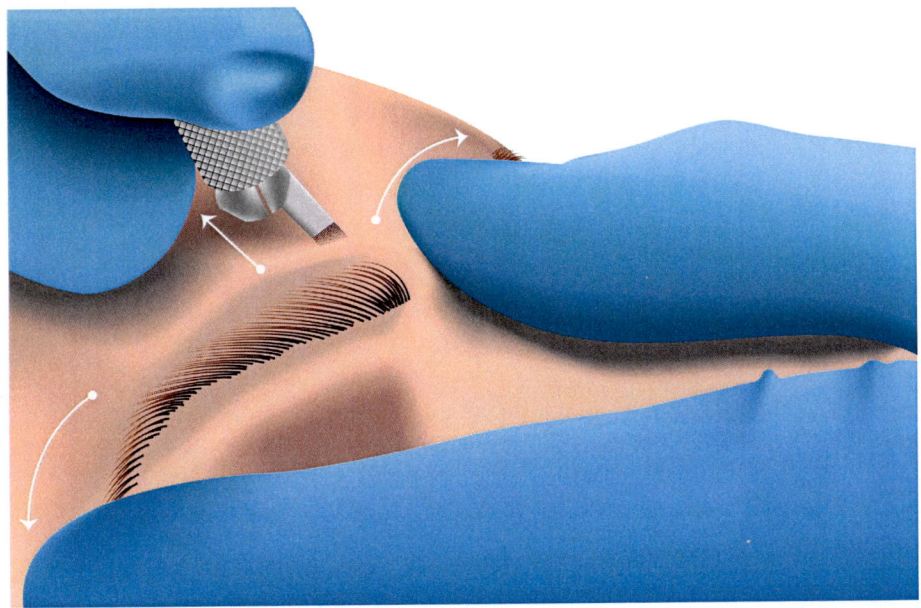

Hold your blade the way you would a pen, applying the same amount of pressure as you would if you were writing. A common beginner's mistake is to apply too much pressure. If you do, your strokes will either blur or heal cool, so watch your depth. On the other hand, if you go too shallowly, you will only land in the dermis and the strokes won't stay.

Every client skin is different and has different thicknesses. Often the skin will be thinner at the tail of the brow and thicker at the bulb, so that the pressure needs to be adjusted as you work.

Older skin is thinner than younger skin, so with older clients you will need to adjust the pressure. Wear a headlamp in order to really gauge the depths of the cuts you are making.

Skin comes in four thicknesses- Super-thin, thin, regular and thick.

Knowing the skin and microblading to the tolerance level of that part of the skin, will help you microblade to the proper level without overworking the skin, giving you better results.

Check your needles before starting every session. A damaged or misaligned needle can cause damage and scarring to the skin and will yield poor results. There are 2 ways to check:

1. Take a picture of the blade with your phone, then zoom in on the picture.
2. Use a loupe or magnifier.

A sign that you've hit the proper depth (what is known as "the sweet spot") is when you see a fine channel or split in the skin, often times marked by fine pinpoint bleeding.

- While microblading, you need to look very carefully in order to assess whether or not you are at the correct depth of the skin's dermis (this is where a headlamp is indispensible).

- Work slowly. It's important to use a slow pace in order to see the fine grooves. Don't hurry or try to speed up the process as your work will suffer. When you make your strokes slowly, you will be better able to determine the correct depth as you go and you will be more precise. Train yourself to make your strokes slowly.

- Not all skin types bleed

- Keep your fingers and wrist loose. Try not to tense up.

- Sensitive skin will bleed easier, in which case, you will need to lighten your pressure to prevent more bleeding. Too much bleeding will dilute the color.

- Every stroke should have a curve. Do not make straight strokes.

- Strokes should be positioned closely and creatively.

- Make sure your blade is in full contact with the skin and fully upright, not leaning to the left or right. If your blade tilts, it will create blurry lines and your strokes will not be clean. In order to get sharp, clean strokes, the blade must enter the skin at a perfect 90-degree angle with all the needles touching the skin.

- To create extra definition, touch the tips of your already created strokes with your blade and pigment. Gently pushing your blade in the opposite direction of your stroke using a slight forward motion. This is a 'barely there' motion. This technique is especially good for the areas where the client is more bald of hairs.

- A common problem with beginner's strokes is that they will disappear, only to reappear later in the healing process. This is caused by going too deep and by applying uneven pressure.

It's important to follow through the strokes with the same even pressure from beginning to end of stroke. Aim for consistency throughout the stroke. Consistency is the most important and most difficult thing to achieve when microblading.

- Very dark or oily skin runs the risk of having it's strokes turn powdery and the lines blurring—Make shorter strokes further apart at the first session and refine at top up session. Very dark or oily skin does better with a harder blade.

- Reduce blade pressure the last third of the brow (the tail).

Tina Davies, a seasoned microblade technician who is an artist and a trainer, has some wonderful YouTube videos on microblading you might want to watch. I personally use and love Tina's line of disposable microblading tools called Harmony. I also highly recommend her line of practice pads called "Angie" which are the only practice pads that tell you if you are using the right amount of pressure. They are unlike any other pads I've encountered.

Tina says,

"Do not apply pressure. As long as the skin is stretched nice and tight (the 3-point stretch) and you're holding your blade nice and straight, then you can let the needles do the work. You are simply guiding the needles."

Here's a wonderful article Tina Davies wrote on microblading:

ARTICLE

Microblading top technical skills:
Stretch, Angle and Slow-Flow

POSTED BY: TINA DAVIES

Microblading top technical skills: STRETCH, ANGLE AND SLOW-FLOW

Microblading is the newest entrant in permanent cosmetics and has been gaining in popularity over the last 2 years. Artists love the idea of tattooing the way they naturally draw and not having to worry about cumbersome wires, power supplies and vibrations.

The technique is very artistic and intuitive; allowing the artist's design to "flow" from her mind to the canvas of the skin. It's not surprising that artists worldwide have quickly embraced microblading and clients are asking for it by name.

There are many challenges in performing microblading properly to obtain the best results. Like any technical skill, proper form is paramount.

In this article, I will share my top 6 technical skills that artists must work at through endless repetition in order to master microblading.

1. Stretch
Hands-down the most important factor in getting great strokes is making great stretches. The key to getting a proper stretch is to flatten

the skin in 3 opposing directions. This is called a 3-point stretch. The stretching hand (the hand without tool) should be placed strategically along the client's forehead to pin the skin down and spread it apart in small, taut stretches. This forms 2 of the 3 points. Now, at the same time, the pinky of working hand must stretch in an opposing direction to complete the 3-point stretch. Just when you think you can't get the skin any flatter, you're almost there. Remember, when the skin is flat, the stroke will be clean since the surface is void of wrinkles and bounce.

2. Depth

The most common question I get asked by artists is about depth. Depth is critical because if you go too shallowly, you will only land in the epidermis, and the color won't stay. If you go too deep, you can cause scarring and the color will heal too ashy. So how do you figure out the perfect depth? The truth is, it's very tricky as every client has a different skin thickness and often, the skin will be much thinner at the tail of the brows than the bulb of the brow. In order for the color to stay, you'll need to microblade to the upper dermis, but not further. A tell-tale sign that you've hit the upper dermis or the "sweet spot", is when you see slight channel in the skin, oftentimes marked by pinpoint bleeding. I talk a lot about microblading to the proper depth and how it relates to the thickness of the client's skin.

3. Read the skin

In my experience, skin comes in 4 thickness varieties: super-thin, thin, regular and thick. You need to understand the tolerance level of the skin to understand it's breaking point. This knowledge will be gained through experience and will help you to understand the proper depth in which to microblade. Imagine two scenarios: slicing a tissue paper and slicing paper towel. When you become familiar working with different skin types, you start to understand if you need to treat your canvas like a tissue paper or a paper towel. Knowing the skin and microblading to the tolerance level of that skin type will help you microblade to the proper level without overworking the skin. Less trauma = better results.

4. Consistency

In microblading, the tortoise always wins. It's very important to use a slow, steady and consistent pace. Not only should you concentrate on making each stroke slowly, you should be acutely aware of the pace of the entire procedure. Don't get caught up in a speed trap and accelerate your work as you progress as your results will suffer. With each case, you will encounter challenges like bleeding, lax skin, or thick patches of hair and the best way to deal with these challenges is to work at a slow consistent pace. When you stroke slowly, you will work with more precision and overcome these types of obstacles. Focus on making each stroke count. Remember, slow and steady wins the race.

5. Angle

The biggest mistake I see people make is in this category. Pay close attention to the angle the blade enters the skin. The needle MUST enter in an upright position and not at an angle. If you look at the side profile of a high quality microblading hairstroke, you will see that the needle penetrates the skin at a 90-degree angle with full contact of all needles touching the skin. Imagine trying to cut a piece of paper with your scissors on an angle, it's not very effective. Microblading is similar. If you are not penetrating the skin with a perpendicular angle, the quality of the stroke will be compromised and hair strokes will be fuzzy.

6. Follow-through

It's important to finish each stroke evenly with the same speed and pressure. You never want to use two (or more) strokes to represent a single strand. Some strokes will be longer than others, so make sure you finish each one and follow through. Take your time here and work slowly to be consistent and precise.

Gaining proficiency at microblading requires a tremendous commitment to consistency and detail and by repetitive practice, you will build the required muscle memory.

So remember: STRETCH, ANGLE, & SLOW-FLOW.

A word about training: through proper training and dedication to continuing education, you can obtain the theory, background and skills that are required for beautiful results. Prior to committing to any training courses, I strongly recommend artists to interview their training instructors by phone or in person as it will be the one of the most important investments one will ever make on their path to success. Professional instructors are never bothered by this process as the good ones are eager to share and mentor students. How many times have you heard of people retaking basic fundamental courses over and over again after being disappointed with inadequate training? If you do your homework upfront and select a good trainer, you should only have to do it once.

Along with proper training, I cannot over stress the importance of a strong knowledge cross contamination and the risks associated with blood-borne pathogens. This education is mandatory for all artists performing any permanent makeup procedures regardless of technique and is critical to protect both the public and the artist. In addition, it is critical to maintain a safe and professional working environment and only use <u>sterile and disposable tools</u>. Building and maintaining a solid reputation depends on your commitment to all safety aspects of this professional trade.

Remember, there are no shortcuts, only hard work. Practice the 6 key steps with a commitment to excellence and I promise you will exceed not only your own expectations, but your client's as well.

Now go and practice!

CHAPTER 11
AFTER CARE

Dry Heal or Wet Heal?

This is another very divided area.

This debate goes from the tattoo artist all the way to the microbladers and everyone in between.

The people who believe in dry healing believe in it wholeheartedly. They are seasoned professionals with years of experience. They know what they're talking about. Unfortunately for those of us that are undecided, so are the people on the wet heal side. Both sides provide very compelling proof of why their method is the only method that works and why their way makes more sense.

One esthetician I spoke to about this subject told me of her theory, which I liked a lot. Since both methods seem to work (and sometimes not work), she believes that it might have to do with their skin types. Maybe, it is better for those with oily skin to dry heal since adding more oil to already oily skin equals too much oil and to wet heal. The people with dry skin may need some moisture to help with healing. That made a lot of sense to me but there is no scientific evidence I can provide you with.

AFTER-CARE

This is a wonderful article written by **Amie Connors** at **Beautiful Ink Tattoos** on how to properly heal a tattoo. With this method, Amie says her clients never scab and never lose pigment. I love that it's based on science:

It's SCIENCE!!! The science of healing...

When the body is tattooed, it's basically injured and we are shoving ink into those punctured wounds. We have created lots of cuts. The body reacts by sending blood and lymph to the injured spots, zipping along with them are macrophages and white blood cells (in the blood).

For about three hours (give or take), a tattooed site gets weepy with the lymph. It's all these things that create a crust or scab because that's what the body wants to do to protect itself from infection. However, nowadays, we can protect the wounds from infections with antibiotic soaps and creams (coconut oil is antibiotic and antibacterial).

Scabs pull out color, so we don't need them. Forever as tattoo artist, we send people away from the shops wrapped in plastic and tell them to take the plastic off in a few hours, wash it gently but well with antibacterial soap and start the regimen of grapeseed or any nut oil, like coconut oil; it's natural, easily absorbed into the skin and have many healing benefits. By having it wrapped, prevents the body fluids from drying out and creating the beginning of a scab in those ever so important first few hours.

Well, we certainly can't send our clients home with their heads wrapped in plastic wrap, so you can always put a layer of a&d or aquaphor on the brow. It's a thick enough layer that as the tattooed area is weeping, it will contain that body fluid and it will not dry out. In these important first few hours, clients are instructed not to touch it, and 3 hours later, to wash their brows gently, removing all traces of A&D or aquaphor with the antibacterial soap. Pat dry with a paper towel, then apply a thin layer of coconut oil or your favorite oil. The whole point is to not let them dry out completely and let the body heal. So after the three hour beginning step, they wash at night with the antibacterial soap and moisturize it with the coconut oil. They are to keep doing this until they've healed. They'll know when they've healed because their skin will be soft again with no flaking.

Now, why not healing with a petroleum or thick non-breathable gel layer?

The skin needs air. It is a semi-permeable organ and by putting on the layer of A&D or Vaseline or aquaphor while it's healing, it is preventing the very necessary thing needed to heal properly.... Air.

So how do you keep it moisturized, but not suffocated? Coconut oil or any nut oil, This is the best way to heal a tattoo and not get scabbing.

This goes for all forms of tattooing: powder as well as strokes (micro-bladed and machined.)

A tattoo is a tattoo.
It is biological science.

Makes a lot of sense.

Then there is this method which is a dry heal method:

Water or any other liquids cannot come in contact with the affected area for 7 days after microblading, even a small drop will expand a wound and a scab will appear.

Disinfect the affected area with a small amount (one spray on a cotton round for both brows) of recommended disinfectant 2-4 times a day. If your skin is oily, make sure you keep your brows clean and dry. You can disinfect more times if needed. If your skin is dry, choose a non-alcohol based disinfectant to avoid additional dryness, you will only want to disinfect 2-3 times a day, over disinfecting will cause dryness.

Examples: alcohol-based disinfectant is a cutasept, otctenidine based products such as octenisept or octidept won't cause itching (70% alcohol based)

If itching occurs, you can use Bactine, and it will also disinfect the area. Bactine contains lidocaine and benzalkonium chloride.

If dryness occurs and ONLY AFTER the 4th day, you can disinfect the area by using a small amount of coconut or grape seed oil. Make sure your brows are not greasy, just slightly moist; no residue of oil should appear.

* After 7 days, you can use a gentle soap or non-greasy cleanser to keep your brows clean.

* Do not use any other ointment or creams with vitamins or antibiotics on brows.

* No sunbathing, or tanning for 4 weeks.

* Do not scratch, touch or sleep on your brows for at least 2 weeks

* No heavy workouts for 10 days. Avoid sweating.

* Avoid Petroleum Jelly or Vaseline during your healing period. Anything with a petroleum base can cause a reaction, crusting, scabbing and sweating, so the skin is not able to breathe.

* It normal to see a little bit of flaking, but not scabbing.

* If you keep your brows clean and dry, only a thin film (not a scab) will appear after 4-7 days. It will peel off itself in 7-10 days (do NOT peel it off). After the film peels off, you can still feel some dryness, in this case clean or disinfect the area with a small amount of coconut or grape seed oil. Be careful with any cleaning in the affected area. The full healing period is 28-45 days.

* If there is any contact with water, sebum or sweat, the expand and cause a scab. The scab will result in

peeling of the pigment. If you scratch the scab, a scar or white spot can appear and no pigment will be left.

* Everyone's skin heals differently. It is important to remember that this is a two-part process and the second touch-up will complete the procedure.

Whichever way you choose to heal your client's brows, these are the points everyone agrees on:

* Absolutely never try to fix or add strokes during the healing process. (This can cause permanent scars).

* No creams, makeup or products on treated area for a minimum of 10 days.

* 4-5 hours after the procedure, clean the area with sterile water and a cotton pad or gauze (debatable: using a mild cleanser or antibiotic soap).

* Avoid heavy sweating for the first 10 days.

* No rubbing, picking or scratching of the treated area. Let any scabbing or dry skin naturally exfoliate off. Picking can and will cause loss of pigment.

* Avoid direct sun exposure or tanning for 3-4 weeks after procedure.

* No facials, botox, microdermabrasion, laser or chemical treatments for 4 weeks after procedure.

* Avoid sleeping on your face for first 10 days.

* No Retin-A, Renova, Alpha Hydroxy or Glycolic Acids ever on microbladed brows

Lightening/Removal Client After-Care

It is critical to follow all aftercare instructions to prevent complications, scarring and to achieve optimum results. Please read carefully.

1. KEEP AREA CLEAN and open to the air. Do not cover with a Band-Aid or anything else, leave open to air. Air/oxygen provides good and faster healing. You should not be touching the area at all, but if you find yourself needing to, please make sure your hands are exceptionally clean.

2. DO NOT SOAK the treated area in water. You can shower as normal, but keep the area out of the shower spray the best you can and do not let the area stay wet for more than a few minutes.

3. NO BATHING, SWIMMING, SAUNAS, HOT TOBS, TANNING, OR INTENSE EXERCISE.

4. DO NOT disrupt the scabbing process (i.e. no picking, scratching, etc.) All scabbing needs to fall off naturally. If you force or pick a scab off, you will disrupt the process and possibly cause scarring.

5. TREAT AREA WITH TLC. DO NOT DO ANYTHING AT ALL THAT COULD CAUSE ISSUE OR PROBLEMS TO THE TREATED AREA. IF YOU ARE NOT SURE OR HAVE ANY QUESTIONS, PLEASE CALL OR EMAIL US.

6. ONCE ALL SCABBING HAS NATURALLY FALLEN OFF, apply one drop Vitamin E Oil 4 to 6 times throughout the day for a minimum of 4 weeks, or until next lightening session. DO NOT start applying the Vitamin E oil UNTIL all scabbing has completely fallen off. It is our goal to keep the area as dry as possible until all scabs have naturally fallen off.

- It is important to the process and integrity of the skin that 8 full weeks of healing take place before another lightening session can be done, no exceptions.

- Lightening and/or removing unwanted pigment is a long process and patience is required. This is true whether you are choosing a lightening product service or laser. Please be patient and give the process a fair chance to work. Expect visible and wanted results in 3 to 6 sessions. How many sessions needed will depend on how saturated the pigment is, how deep it was implanted and how much needs to be removed for the desired result. In many cases, only a percentage of the density needs to be lightened/removed and then we can continue the correction process by color correcting. In those cases, where we have pigment misplaced or in an unwanted area, color correcting will not be an option and removing as much of the pigment as possible will be our ultimate goal.

- Results cannot be foreseen, predicted or guaranteed.

CHAPTER 12
THE HEALING PROCESS

It is definitely a process. The clients almost always gets nervous during this time and will need some hand holding no matter how much you explain the process. It's understandable. Looking in the mirror and seeing yourself with eyebrows that are too dark and too thick is a scary prospect that would send even the most confident person into bouts of uncertainty.

I think there's not a client out there who didn't wonder, during the healing process, if they hadn't just made a huge mistake. Fortunately, by the time the healing process is done and they come back for the touch up, they are happy, relaxed and fully confident.

WHAT TO EXPECT DURING THE HEALING PROCESS

Your new temporary eyebrows will go through several phases during the healing cycle.

Initially, your brows may seem to be too red and too large. Don't be alarmed. We have just worked the skin and it is natural for it to be red and swollen. It will calm down in a day or so.

The pigment will appear very sharp and dark immediately after the procedure. This is because the pigment is still sitting on top of your skin, and has not settled in completely. The color of the pigment will soften gradually. The scabbing process will also make the brows appear dark. Stay calm, all of this will lighten within a week or so. The color will eventually be 30- 50% lighter and the brow will be 20-30% smaller when fully healed.

Once the healing of the skin starts taking place, it will look like dandruff flakes or dry skin. This might give you the impression that the color pigment is fading too quickly, however, this is just superficial color and dry skin being naturally removed/from your eyebrows.

Some strokes will disappear and re-appear in 2 or 3 weeks. Not all strokes will remain. It is perfectly natural to lose between 10-15% of your strokes, they will get replaced at the top up or second session.

You may feel some itching, please try to resist. If you find yourself unable to resist itching, you may apply some Bactine to the area for relief.

Once all scabbing has naturally fallen off and skin is healed, you may apply vitamin E oil to the brow a few times a day, until it is time for your second session.

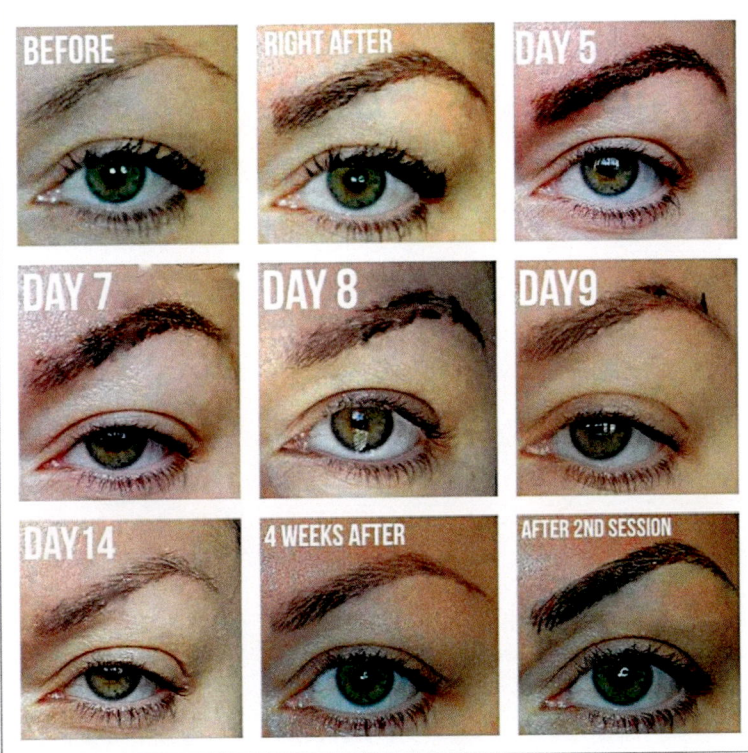

Picture provided by brow artist Joanna Bieszczad

Day 1: OMG! I'm in love with my new brows. Thank you!

Day 2-4: I don't like this color, it's too dark.

Day 5-7: Oh, no! My brows are scabbing and falling off.

Day 8-10: WTF? My brows are gone!

Day 14-28: Thanks God my brows are coming back! Still looking patchy and uneven.

Day 42 (after touch up): Aww, they're beautiful! I love them! Thanks again!

CHAPTER 13
COURSES AND TRAINERS

Finding the right course and the right trainer is the first and most important step to take. There's nothing worse than paying thousands of dollars for a course that you feel was not the right one for you.

How do you find the right course for you? The facebook groups are a brilliant place to look. You get to hear other people's recommendations and experiences. You can ask them all the questions you want, and yet, there are still no guarantees. There are always so many you hadn't heard about before you took your course. Location is often a consideration, so is the price.

You can find courses ranging in price from $2,500 all the way to $10,000. Since everyone learns differently and has different requirements, you will have to do your own research but here is a list of all the trainers I could find.

You decide who is best for you.

ARTICLE

What to Look for in a Microblading Training Provider

Vogue Brows / July 24, 2016

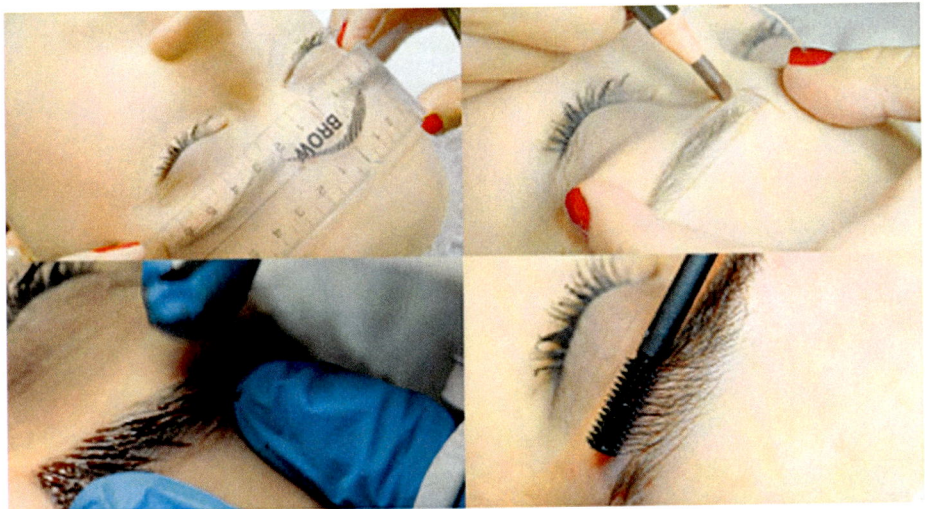

Choosing a Training provider is an important first step and can be a daunting experience, especially if you have no idea what to look for. There are so many trainers out there, some great, some not so great. How do we know the difference when we don't know microblading? Here is an article written by Vogue Brows in South Africa that gives you pointers with what to look for in a training.

But be sure to do your research carefully.

THE MICROBLADING TRAINING PROCESS EXPLAINED

Although Microblading is actually a form of Permanent Makeup, it should be treated as a separate and completely different form of art. When comparing PMU done by machine with Microblading, it becomes apparent that Microblading allows for thinner, more natural looking and realistic hair strokes. It's worth mentioning that Microblading is a skill requiring months of practice before starting to charge your clients for the procedure. It is vital to achieve clean, crisp strokes and good pigment retention. Drawing strokes mimicking perfectly curved hairs is extremely complex and requires a lot of practice. It is also very challenging to work on different faces, so to immediately practice on live models is rather irresponsible. We advise practicing with the trainer present and then to practice on artificial skin before working with live models. To truly obtain the Microblading expertise, 2-3 months of practicing is required.

One should be capable of:

- Identifying skin type
- Choosing the right brow shape for face type
- Proper numbing techniques
- Stretching the skin correctly whilst working
- Creating different natural strokes
- Know the correct depth for each stroke
- Creating symmetry of both brows
- Calculating the eyebrow shape based on the Golden Mean Ratio method
- Accurately select color pigments and modifier
- Understanding proper after care

http://www.voguebrows.com/information/look-training-provider

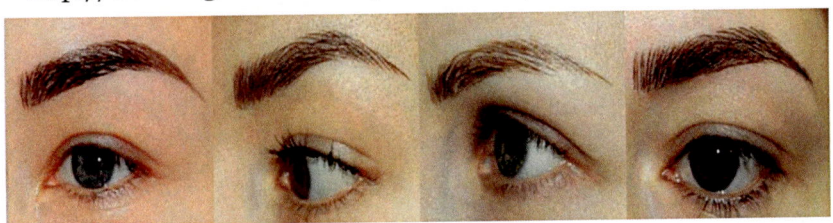

WHEN DOING YOUR RESEARCH FOR THE ULTIMATE MICROBLADING COURSE, LOOK FOR THE FOLLOWING:

Curriculum

We believe that it is important to have a very strong curriculum that covers everything there is to know about Microblading and safe practicing! Let's break it down:

1. Structure of the skin
Understanding the layers of the skin, the different types of skin and of the different penetration techniques is very important. Make sure your training covers that in detail. It is also of the utmost importance to understand the different skin types and which products / equipment to use in order to achieve the best healing results. Ask your prospective trainers how much time is spent on skin.

2. Facial areas, features & proportion
It is vital to understand the facial areas, features and proportions in order to offer your client a custom designed eyebrow shape that will compliment and frame her face beautifully. Make sure your training will provide you with some guidance as to which eyebrow shapes compliment which faces.

3. Eyebrow structure & measurement

This is where a lot of artists/students get scared, hearing the word measuring! It is not rocket science – well almost! Measuring is the most important step when it comes to designing the ultimate eyebrow. It's important to learn the various methods of eyebrow measuring to ensure students find one that they are completely comfortable with. "Eyebrows are not identical twins; they are sisters – but they should also not be distant cousins".

4. Safety & Sanitation

Safety and Sanitation first! Protecting yourself as well as your clients is of the utmost importance! We cannot stress enough how careful one should be when working with blood and cutting into the skin. Look for a training that promotes safe practices and proper hygiene when it comes to the Microblading procedure.

5. Colour study

An in depth section on colour study is crucial to assist students in choosing the best colour for each individual client. Understanding the Fitzpatrick scale to best determine the client's undertones and which modifiers to use for each Fitzpatrick type.

6. Blades Types and Their Uses

I don't need to tell you how important it is to understand the different blade types; their purposes on which skin types. It almost goes without saying, knowing this information is a must, and yet, many courses do not cover this very important element. Make sure the training you choose does.

7. Anaesthetics

Anaesthetics should be taken seriously in order to avoid any mishaps! Students need to know the following:

- Overview
- Indications

- Dosage Guidelines and Administrative Techniques
- Mechanism of Action
- Absorption
- Adverse Effects
- Allergic Reactions

8. Different Techniques Available

Even though 3D and 6D eyebrows look very similar, there is one important difference: The thickness of the blade. Blades used for 6D are smaller/thinner in diameter to the blades used for the 3D technique, therefore creating a thinner 'cut/stroke' in the skin and ultimately resulting in an ultra-thin crisp and clean stroke. Then there is the oh-so-popular ombre/shading and powder technique. Does your training provide this information?

Everyone one is different and will have different needs and ways of learning but these 12 microblading subjects are non-negotiable. These are the basics every good microblading technician must know. Admittedly, it's hard to get everything you need to know in one training, and learning comes in levels, so what you need to know as a beginner is different than what you'll need to know as an advanced technician, which is why on-going education is a must.

Try not to let price be your guide. If you go with the $1,500 course because it's more affordable, but afterwards you still don't have answers to your questions and you're left with not enough confidence to do anyone, or worse, you do, it will not have been a good deal after all. It will always end up costing you more on the back end. It will cost you in time and mistakes, which equals to loss of clients and loss of income.

I have a saying, "It's expensive to be poor," meaning, it always costs more in the long run to pay less in the short run.

If you can't afford the right course at the moment, you might be better off waiting, borrowing or making payments than to take a lesser costing course.

Then again, don't automatically assume the expensive course is a good course just because it's expensive. Do your research. Try to speak to people who've done the course, it's easy now with social media. If you want to be sure you'll get the absolute best training without the guesswork, come to Vogue Brows in South Africa. We'll make sure you leave with all the knowledge you need to be a confident and skilled microblading technician.

I'd like to add a note here; When choosing a trainer/training, inquire into what line of pigments they recommend and endorse and how much training do they provide for this line of pigments. Is this a good line of colors for you? Look into it. The line of pigments you start out with will have everything to do with the amount of success you will have with the eyebrows you create and is an important part of your microblading education.

Following is a list of Trainers and Training facilities from around the world.

Academy of Advanced Cosmetics- Gorgia, USA
Academia Biotek – Toscany, IT
Advanced Aesthetics International- UK*
American Beauty Institute*
Baltic Brows*
Bangkok Beauty Academy
Bare Face Beauty- Wilmslow, Cheshire
Beau Institute of Permanent & Corrective Cosmetics- NJ, USA
Beauty Annex- N.Y. & Louisiana
Beauty Training Academy- Cindy Mackenzie- UK
Beyond the Brows - London
Biotek – UK
Biotouch*
Brigit Microblading & PMU- London
Broadway Lash and Blade Academy*
Brow Design Microblading Academy*
Center For Permanent Makeup- Canada
Colett Academy- AZ
Dallas Skin Institute- Dallas, TX
Daria Chuprys- Beverly Hills
Deluxe Brows- San Diego
Dermagraph – London
Elite Microblading Academy – Los Angeles
Endless Beauty- Florida
Epibrow*
Everlasting Brows*
Eye Design – New York
Flirt and Flutter Make Up Academy
Glamore Aesthetics, LLD- UK*
Institute of Beauty and Hollistic Training- Dublin
Guru Brows- Online Training**

Images Enterprises- Tucson, AZ
Imperia Beauty- Marbella, Spain
Irena Chen- World Microblading*
J'adore microblading academy*
Katerina Zapletalova – Hereford, UK
Kevin Chen- Guangzhou, China
KS Brow Academy
Lash Art University- Ukraine
Lash Forever- Canada
Lavish Beauty Brow- FL
Laura Kay London- England
Lukx Brows- Online Training**
Luxury Lash Lounge- Atlanta, GA
Luxus BeautyLine Microblading Academy- Germany
Mary Ritcherson- Tampa, Florida
Microblading Technician Program- Canada
Microblading Training Academy- UT
Microblading Training USA
Natural Look Institute- San Diego
Next Door Spa- Dublin, Ireland
Nouveau Contour*
Occhi Institute- Illinois
Oxana Dillmann Microblading Academy- Germany
Pefect Eyebrows - Texas
Phi Brows – Microblading Academy by Branko Babic
Pigmenta Permante Cosmetics- MA
Plaza Di Laura Academy- Sweden
Princess Brows – Hong Kong
Prive Microblading Academy
Pro Brows – London- Helsinki- Switzerland- Austria
Sandra Opul Permanent Makeup- London
Sculpting Microblading by Tiffiny Luong
Shador- Online Training**
Sleek Brows*

Soft tap*
Sviatoslav Otchenash – Germany
Sydney Cosmetic Tattoo – Australia
Teryn Darling- Nevada
Tina Davies- Toronto
The Jhon-Jhon Institute – Definition Brows
The Esthetic Institute Training Center- Canada
The Look Microblading Training- TX
The Urban Beauty Lounge- South Africa
3D Brows Academy*
Unique Contour spmu Artists & Training Institute-UK
Versailles Medical Spa- NY
Vesta Academy – Ft Lauderdale, FL
Vogue Brows- South Africa

This list in no way claims to be complete
They are not in one location, they travel to different locations
** Not recommended for beginners. Good for continuing education

Made in the USA
San Bernardino, CA
18 April 2017